MONTVILLE TWP. PUBLIC LIBRARY
90 HORSENECK ROAD
MONTVILLE, NJ 07045

ON LINE

JBIOG
Cohen 07-2-08
Hill, Anne E.

Sasha Cohen

Montville Township Public Library
90 Horseneck Road
Montville, N.J. 07045-9626
973-402-0900
<u>Library Hours</u>

Monday	10 a.m.-9 p.m.
Tuesday	10 a.m.-9 p.m.
Wednesday	1 p.m.- 9 p.m.
Thursday	10 a.m.- 9 p.m.
Friday	10 a.m.- 5 p.m.
Saturday	10 a.m.- 5 p.m.
Sunday	1 p.m.- 5 p.m.

Closed Sundays July & August
see website   www.montvillelib.org

MONTVILLE TWP. PUBLIC LIBRARY
90 HORSENECK ROAD
MONTVILLE, NJ 07045

ON LINE

Sasha Cohen

Read all of the books in this exciting,
action-packed biography series!

Hank Aaron	*Wayne Gretzky*
Muhammad Ali	*Derek Jeter*
Lance Armstrong	*Sandy Koufax*
David Beckham	*Michelle Kwan*
Barry Bonds	*Mickey Mantle*
Roberto Clemente	*Jesse Owens*
Sasha Cohen	*Alex Rodriguez*
Joe DiMaggio	*Wilma Rudolph*
Tim Duncan	*Annika Sorenstam*
Dale Earnhardt Jr.	*Ichiro Suzuki*
Doug Flutie	*Jim Thorpe*
Lou Gehrig	*Tiger Woods*

SPORTS HEROES AND LEGENDS™

Sasha Cohen

by Anne E. Hill

Twenty-First Century Books/Minneapolis

For Abby Jane,
The daughter I always wanted and am overjoyed to have.
Love, Mommy

Copyright © 2007 by Lerner Publishing Group, Inc.

Sports Heroes and Legends™ is a trademark of Barnes and Noble, Inc.

Used with permission from Barnes and Noble, Inc.

All rights reserved. International copyright secured. No part of this book may be reproduced, stored in a retrieval system, or transmitted in any form or by any means—electronic, mechanical, photocopying, recording, or otherwise—without the prior written permission of Lerner Publishing Group, Inc., except for the inclusion of brief quotations in an acknowledged review.

Twenty-First Century Books
A division of Lerner Publishing Group, Inc.
241 First Avenue North
Minneapolis, MN 55401 U.S.A.

Website address: www.lernerbooks.com

Cover photograph:
© Getty Images

Library of Congress Cataloging-in-Publication Data

Hill, Anne E., 1974–
      Sasha Cohen / by Anne E. Hill.
            p.   cm. — (Sports heroes and legends)
      Includes bibliographical references and index.
      ISBN 978–0–8225–7164–3 (lib. bdg. : alk. paper)
      1. Cohen, Sasha, 1984– —Juvenile literature. 2. Figure skaters—United States—Biography—Juvenile literature. 3. Women figure skaters—United States—Biography—Juvenile literature. I. Title.
GV850.C65H55 2007
796.91'2092—dc22 [B]   2006101704

Manufactured in the United States of America
1 2 3 4 5 6 – JR – 12 11 10 09 08 07

0 1021 0217088 7

09/2007
Lev
8 29.27

Contents

The Best in the United States

Winded, her arms and legs aching, Sasha Cohen beamed into the stands of the packed Savvis Center Arena in St. Louis, Missouri. She had finally done it. She had skated a virtually error-free long program at the 2006 U.S. Figure Skating Championships, or Nationals. Although her fate was in the hands of the judges, she had been first heading into the evening's long program. She would likely be going home with the gold medal.

Sasha took a deep bow. Then she collected some of the many flowers and stuffed animals that fans had thrown onto the ice. Despite her feeling of accomplishment, Sasha knew the performance hadn't been her best. She'd struggled on the landing of her triple toe jump. But unlike her competitors, she had not fallen down. She anxiously awaited her scores in a section next to the skating rink known as the kiss-and-cry area. Sasha wanted to find out if she would finally take home a gold after so many second-place finishes in previous competitions.

This year's Nationals were even more important than usual. The top finishers would represent the United States at the 2006 Olympic Games in Turin, Italy. Sasha had finished fourth at the 2002 Olympic Games in Salt Lake City, Utah, after a nasty fall. She wanted to prove she could skate well enough to medal at the Olympics.

With so much riding on her performance at Nationals, twenty-one-year-old Sasha made sure to take good care of herself in the weeks leading up to the competition. She trained for hours with her coach, John Nicks. She got lots of rest and ate well. Despite her careful preparation, Sasha still caught the flu less than a week before Nationals began. "I was like . . . I can't be sick," Sasha said. "I'm taking every single vitamin . . . going to bed every night at 9:30. Why is this happening?"

But Sasha was used to working through illness and injury. She knew she couldn't give up. She stayed in bed all weekend and almost missed her Monday flight from her home in California to St. Louis. On her arrival, she crawled into the hotel bed and caught up on the first season of one of her favorite TV shows, *Desperate Housewives.* When she emerged from her room to practice on Tuesday, she couldn't complete her program. She was uncoordinated and dizzy. She couldn't land any of her jumps. Instead of panicking, she decided to take things one day at a time.

By Thursday evening, the night of the nearly three-minute short program, Sasha was no longer dizzy. But she was weak and slower than usual on the ice. She was determined to get through the two minutes and forty-nine seconds of her routine. She did more than that.

Clad in a blue skating dress with a colorful skirt, Sasha performed to "Dark Eyes," a Russian folk song. She nailed a triple lutz–double toe loop combination in the early moments of her routine. She went on to complete a triple flip, a sit spin, a double axel, a spiral sequence (graceful balances on one leg), a beautiful layback spin, footwork, and a final spin. Throughout the routine, Sasha displayed her signature flexibility and lightness on her blades. "I was pretty happy with that," Sasha told reporters after she left the ice. "I really enjoyed the performance tonight. Had a week of unknowns, being in bed with the flu. I'm really well trained. This is not half as good as I've been doing in training."

Even though she had skated better in practice, Sasha blew past her competitors in the short program. She gained a comfortable lead over other Olympic hopefuls Kimmie Meissner and Emily Hughes. (Sasha's biggest competition, reigning national champion Michelle Kwan, had a groin injury and was unable to compete at Nationals.)

After her promising start at Nationals, Sasha rested instead of pushing herself on the ice. She wanted to be ready for her more strenuous long program, which lasted four minutes. She needed to be in top form to secure her place on the Olympic team and to prove to her critics that she could skate a clean long program.

For years, Sasha had been criticized for choking at big events, losing the gold in the long program because of a fall or mistake late in the routine. "Having skated in Michelle's shadow for so long, Sasha doesn't tend to get the credit for all she has accomplished," said Coach Nicks. "She's been criticized a lot for skating badly, but you don't win silver medals if you skate badly."

Sasha had a gold medal on the line as she took the ice on the night of the long program. She skated to music from the 1968 film *Romeo and Juliet.* Her filmy, pale yellow skating dress matched the music's romantic mood. And more important, her costume matched the gold medal that hung from her neck moments later.

Sasha received a total score of 199.18 for her short and long programs. The score was twenty-eight points higher than that of the second-place finisher, Kimmie Meissner. It was also Sasha's highest point total ever. She was the best in the United States and headed to the Olympic Games. Her fifteen years of training were paying off. "I've evolved in a way, I think," Sasha said. "I've learned to just enjoy it. I feel lucky to do what I do. I'm going to go out there, trust my training, and have fun. I hope my time is now."

Chapter One

Ice Cream and Ice-Skating

Sasha was born Alexandra Pauline Cohen in Los Angeles, California, on October 26, 1984. She was the firstborn child of her parents, Galina and Roger Cohen.

Galina was born in Odessa, Ukraine. She had trained in gymnastics and ballet before moving to the United States with her family when she was sixteen years old. Roger, a native Californian, was also an athlete. He had studied skiing at the American College of Switzerland. The two were attending college in San Diego, California, when they met and fell in love. They married less than one year after meeting. Roger later graduated from the School of Law at the University of California—Berkeley and became a lawyer. Galina began a career in international banking. The arrival of Sasha and her little sister, Natalia (nicknamed Natasha), almost four years later made the Cohens a happy family of four.

Sasha is very close to both sets of grandparents, particularly her mother's parents, Babba (Russian for "Grandma") and Dyed (Russian for "Grandpa"). They lived in San Diego, which is about 130 miles south of Los Angeles. Babba was always cooking or baking and insisting that Sasha and Natasha eat. Unlike Sasha's mother and father, who believed in a diet without a lot of sugar, Babba had no rules about junk food. "I remember her saying, 'Sasha, you cannot have ice cream if you do not finish your doughnut first!'" Sasha recalled.

Ukraine was part of the former Union of Soviet Socialist Republics (U.S.S.R.). The Communist Party controlled the U.S.S.R. from 1922 to 1991, when Communist rule ended and the country split into fifteen independent nations. Although some people in Ukraine speak Russian, the majority speak Ukrainian. Galina speaks Russian, and Sasha can understand Russian, though she doesn't speak it fluently.

With her parents' athletic backgrounds, it was no surprise that young Sasha showed promise in sports. Or maybe Galina and Roger were just anxious to get their rambunctious preschooler out of the house for a few hours a week. As a youngster, Sasha always had lots of energy to burn. Four-year-old

Sasha started taking gymnastics lessons at Flair's Gym in her hometown of Pasadena.

Although she was still a young child, Sasha began intense training. She learned moves on the floor as well as how to use the apparatuses—beam, vault, and uneven parallel bars. Her favorite activity, however, was jumping on the trampoline. (Perhaps Sasha liked the sensation of flying, which she seems to do on the ice.) Her teachers were always telling her to get off the trampoline and move to the next piece of gym equipment.

As a little girl, Sasha was spirited and sometimes got into trouble. Her parents often put her in "time-outs" as punishment. She once tried to negotiate her way out of her time-out, but she wasn't successful!

Sasha discovered more at Flair's Gym than a love for the trampoline. She also learned she had a competitive spirit. At the end of practice, the coaches would toss a trinket, such as a piece of costume jewelry or a key chain, into a foam ball pit and let the kids dive in to see who could find it first. The winner kept the prize. If little Sasha wasn't the winner each week, she was disappointed and even more determined the next time they got to play. She also got a glimpse of the trophies gymnasts who trained at Flair's had won. She decided she would like to win trophies of her own someday.

Sasha is a common Russian nickname for Alexandra.

At age seven, Sasha had never set foot on the ice, but she was training three hours a day as a gymnast. She had graduated to a more advanced level and was learning dangerous tricks. One day in 1992, Galina watched her young daughter lose her concentration and narrowly miss being injured. She decided it was time for a change. One of Sasha's friends from gymnastics also ice-skated. The friend's grandmother suggested to Galina that Sasha try skating too. Galina liked the idea. As a girl, she had wanted to learn to skate. Unfortunately, the rink in her hometown had been under construction for more than ten years, so she had never gotten the chance.

Once she began skating, Sasha quickly forgot about gymnastics. "I knew that first day [on the ice] that I wanted to learn more. The cold, the feeling of being out of control, and the bumps and bruises from falling on the ice didn't bother me," she recalled. Sasha found herself begging for lessons and more time on the ice. Galina agreed but also set some ground rules:

no early morning practices (some of the other mothers had their daughters at the rink at 5:30 A.M.) and no competing for a while.

DARLENE SPARKS BELL

One of Sasha's first group skating coaches was Darlene Sparks Bell. Bell had been trained by renowned coach Carlo Fassi (who had coached Olympic gold medalists Dorothy Hamill and Peggy Fleming) and even competed at the National level. Bell believed in Sasha's ability early on and made her first moments on the ice fun and memorable. Even as a champion skater, Sasha still turns to Bell for advice and tips.

So Sasha learned the skating basics and had fun on the ice in group lessons. She tried to be patient, but she noticed that the other skaters already had more experience. Many of them had started skating at age four or five. Sasha was anxious to catch up. She said: "In my group lessons I'd spend a lot of time looking around the rink to see what the more advanced skaters were learning. While I was learning swizzles, waltz jumps, and two-foot spins, my mind was calculating how quickly I could move on to what the 'big girls' were doing. So it was thrilling when I completed the group lessons and my mom put me into my first private classes."

Sasha's first private coach was Russian Victor Yelchin. He insisted she get a real skating dress and her own pair of skates. Sasha had been using rental skates and a stretchy skirt for practices. She was thrilled to go shopping for skating things. (Even as a little girl, Sasha loved to shop.)

Sasha's astrological sign is Scorpio. Scorpios are known for being exciting, magnetic, determined, intuitive, powerful, and passionate.

Galina and Sasha went to the rink's professional shop They chose a beautiful turquoise-and-gold skating dress with three layers of flouncy skirts. When the salesperson brought over the ice skates, Sasha and her mother were confused. None of the boots had any blades. They found out that the blades are sold separately—but they believed this only after opening several boxes to make sure none of the skates had blades attached!

Armed with her own skating dress and skates and a new coach, Sasha felt ready to take her skating to the next level. But she knew very little about the skating levels and how to progress through them. Victor explained that competition can begin as early as three years old.

The United States Figure Skating Association (USFSA), the governing body for U.S. figure skaters, bases its eight levels on skills rather than age. Those levels are pre-preliminary, preliminary, pre-juvenile, juvenile, intermediate, novice, junior, and senior. Each level has its own set of required elements that a skater must perform to advance through the ranks. When skaters move to the next level, they receive a pin that signifies they can compete with other skaters at that level. Skaters who compete at the Olympics, Nationals, and World Championships are all senior-level skaters. Sasha was a juvenile skater, four ranks away from being a senior. She was determined to compete with her peers, who were already doing double jumps while she was still trying to nail her singles.

Victor created Sasha's first program to the music of the opera *Carmen.* Sasha said she can't remember much about the program except that it was a minute and a half long and it had a few jumps, spins, and spirals. But she can recall her first competitions clearly. She loved wearing her mom's lipstick and putting hair spray on her tight ponytail. "The smell of hair spray and the taste of a certain lipstick still make me nervous," Sasha said.

Galina accompanied Sasha to all of her events, while Roger, Natasha, Babba, and Dyed attended the bigger competitions. Sasha loved the all-day events. They included ice-skating, meeting and hanging out with the other young skaters, buying skating items from the vendors at the rink, and going out to dinner afterward.

Sasha treated her younger sister, Natasha, like one of her dolls. Her earliest memory of her sister is of sticking little gift bows on her head!

Even though she had fun at skating events, eight-year old Sasha was becoming more serious about the sport. She wanted to compete against people her own age, which meant she had some catching up to do. In 1993, under Victor's coaching, she perfected the waltz jump, a basic jump that is similar to an axel. The skater takes off from a forward outside edge and does half a rotation in the air. A single axel, by comparison, is one and a half rotations. (A double axel, Sasha's favorite jump and one that all senior ladies must perform, is actually two and a half rotations in the air.) Learning the waltz jump is important because it is the basis for many other jumps.

Just as Sasha was getting used to Victor's coaching and going to competitions, her family decided to move. They were leaving their hometown of Pasadena, California, for Orange County, California. What Sasha didn't realize was that she was moving close to the Ice Capades Chalet, home of famous skating coach John Nicks.

Chapter | Two

Changes

Moving to a new town was exciting and a little scary for Sasha and Natasha. The Cohens rented a house while they built their dream home in Laguna Niguel. Galina worked with an architect so that the house would have everything the family wanted. The house took more than a year to complete. But it had breathtaking views of the canyons and ocean that made it worth the wait.

By 1994 nine-year-old Sasha had begun skating at the Ice Capades Chalet in nearby Costa Mesa. She started training with Yvonne Nicks, wife of coach John Nicks. Yvonne was the official spin coach of the rink. Sasha's spins and speed on the ice improved greatly after a few practice sessions. Because she had been a gymnast, Sasha was very flexible. She could do twists and extensions that many other skaters could not. But her jumps needed more work.

While taking private lessons with Yvonne twice a month, Sasha competed in her first USFSA competition and came in second. It was a promising start, and Sasha was proud of her accomplishment. But she knew she still had a lot to learn.

In addition to jumps and spins, Sasha got an education in boots and blades. She had more than twenty different kinds of boots and fifteen different kinds of blades to choose from. She also had to consider off-ice conditioning (ballet, running, swimming, and other types of exercises) and find time for on-ice practice sessions at crowded rinks.

Because Sasha wanted to practice more than twice a week, she and Galina drove to nearly every rink in Southern California to look for the nicest and least crowded one. Despite having warm weather, California has produced a large number of elite figure skaters. Up-and-comer Michelle Kwan trained at the Ice Castle International Training Center in Lake Arrowhead. (Michelle and Sasha would later compete with each other as senior ladies.) Lake Arrowhead is about eighty miles east of Los Angeles. "Skaters from all over the world would practice [at Ice Castle], and it was inspiring to watch them and practice on the same ice they were skating on," Sasha said in her autobiography.

Whenever she went to Lake Arrowhead, Sasha also enjoyed visiting the local pet store. Each time she went in, she begged Galina for a kitten. Galina finally allowed her to have one for her eleventh birthday. Sasha named the gray tiger-striped cat Meow Meow. Meow Meow later accompanied Sasha to many of her competitions.

Sasha tried to get Natasha to ice-skate. But Natasha always thought the ice was too cold. She pursued her own interests in music, ballet, and poetry instead.

Sasha was beginning to travel to more competitions outside Southern California. She started training with Barbara Brown. She also began taking technical lessons with Roger Bass. He worked with Sasha on her combination jumps (two or more jumps in a row). Sasha finally mastered the difficult single axel and started on her double jumps. She was getting used to falling and being wet and bruised from the ice. But she believed that her work was paying off as she prepared for the 1996 Southwest Pacific Regionals.

The Regionals event was the biggest competition Sasha had ever skated in. She needed a new costume for her routine to *Carmen*. Galina and Sasha chose rich red satin fabric with black chiffon and gold lace for the trimmings. They took the material to a friend of Babba's who made the dress. The resulting costume had six layers of skirts and large sleeves. Although it was beautiful, the dress proved difficult to skate in. "The materials didn't stretch; the sleeves made it hard to move my arms; there were so many skirts," Sasha recalled. "It was definitely a good lesson in how to make a competitive skating dress!"

Despite her stiff costume, Sasha skated well at Regionals. She came in fourth place. At this level of skating, the top four finishers receive medals and stand on the podium (the fourth-place medal is pewter). Sasha loved the feeling of standing with the winners. She vowed to win more often.

SKATING COMPETITIONS

Regionals are the first step for skaters who want to compete at the U.S. National Championships. The top juvenile and intermediate-level skaters from Regionals qualify for an event called Junior Nationals. At the novice, junior, and senior levels, the top four finishers from each region must compete against skaters from other regions at Sectionals. The top four finishers in each of three Sectionals qualify for Nationals.

To make it atop more podiums, Sasha started taking lessons with John Nicks. Several months later, he became her full-time coach. Sasha had become an intermediate-level skater.

But despite being more advanced in her skating skills, Sasha was slightly intimidated by her new coach, whom she always called "Mr. Nicks." Nicks had coached Peggy Fleming and pairs skaters Tai Babilonia and Randy Gardner. His current pupils included pairs skaters Jenni Meno and Todd Sand. British-born Nicks and his sister, Jennifer, had won Britain's only World Pairs Championship in 1953.

Nicks saw tremendous potential in Sasha. Although his other students, such as Naomi Nari Nam, had more jumping skills, Sasha had a poetic style on the ice. Under Nicks's watchful eye, Sasha's skating improved. The twelve-year-old competed at the 1997 Southwest Pacific Regionals. At her first Regionals as an intermediate skater, Sasha came in second place. While intermediate skaters no longer compete at Sectionals, they did in 1997. So Sasha's win qualified her to compete at the 1997 Pacific Coast Sectionals.

---

66 *Sasha is elegance personified. I've said before that she is naturally unable to get into an ugly position. She looks fragile, but that's deceptive; she's a very tough young lady.* **99**

—JOHN NICKS

Sasha was excited to attend her first competition outside of Southern California. She and her mom flew to Salt Lake City, Utah. They stayed in a hotel for the week. Sasha met other young skaters and made new friends. Despite the distractions of traveling for the first time, Sasha skated well and came in fourth place. That year the top four intermediate skaters from the three Sectional events went on to compete at the Junior Olympics, rather than at Junior Nationals. Sasha could hardly wait! She was going to the Junior Olympics!

SKATING FRIENDS

One of Sasha's favorite things about skating is meeting other skaters and making new friends. In the mid-1990s, one of Sasha's best friends was also her biggest competition: Naomi Nari Nam. Naomi also trained with John Nicks. Tiffany Stiegler and her brother, Johnnie, were pairs skaters whom Sasha befriended. When they weren't practicing on the ice or doing schoolwork, Sasha and her friends loved to go out to eat, shop, or just hang out.

Although she was proud to go to the Junior Olympics, Sasha was disappointed to learn that they were being held in Anaheim, not far from her hometown. Sasha wouldn't get to travel to a new city or stay in a hotel for this competition. However, Sasha's father, sister, and grandparents could all watch her skate.

Before the competition, Sasha stepped up her training with Nicks. She was still frustrated that she wasn't able to perform as many jumps as her peers. Most of the female skaters could do a double axel and even land a triple jump. To avoid being intimidated by other skaters, Sasha practiced at her own local rink rather than at the competition ice rink. Keeping her focus was important. Sasha was more nervous than she had ever been at a competition.

Although she skated competently at the Junior Olympics, the other skaters simply had more advanced skills. Sasha came in fifth place. She was a little disappointed but also proud of how far her skating had come in just five years. She set a goal for herself. In three more years, by 2000, she wanted to be a senior skater.

Chapter | Three

Moving through the Ranks

No one could question Sasha's commitment to skating. She was spending more and more time on the ice. Her dream was to make it to the Olympics one day. Before she could make her dream come true, she needed to be a senior-level skater. Since she was still several levels away, Sasha focused on moving through the skating ranks.

When she wasn't training with Nicks at Ice Capades, Sasha was training at Ice Castle, skating and watching the elite skaters. Her friend Allison Larson had moved to Lake Arrowhead, so Sasha spent weekends there learning as much as she could. She took lessons from Irina Rodnina, a Russian pairs coach, as well as Elena Tcherkasskaia, a former Russian ballerina.

But Sasha's visits to Lake Arrowhead weren't all work and no play. Sasha went out to the local Chinese restaurant on Friday nights, had Saturday brunches with other skaters, and even water-skied with the Stiegler family on Saturday after-noons. She tried to strike a good balance between skating and having fun off the ice.

The Sasha Curl

Sasha's incredible flexibility led her to invent her own stunning move on the ice. It's called the Sasha curl. In this move, Sasha lays her head back while she curls one leg up behind her, nearly touching her head—all without using her hands.

Her training had become more intense and painful because she was trying to master the double axel. This jump requires a skater to take off forward from one blade, spin in the air two and a half times, and land on the other blade going backward. Sasha's body was black and blue from taking so many falls on the ice. Her bruises healed a little after she bought some padded shorts. They cushioned her landings when she fell on her hips. Sasha was determined to learn the jump. "[The double axel is] the glass ceiling, the major line. Once you have it, you kind of establish yourself as a skater. If you don't, you can't compete at the upper levels," Sasha explained.

The twelve-year-old was on the ice practicing one day when she had her first bad skating accident. She and one other skater were practicing their jumps. Sasha extended her leg after landing a jump. The other skater was moving backward and jumped right into Sasha's outstretched leg. The skater's blade cut into Sasha's right calf. Sasha ended up with twenty-one stitches in her leg. Although the injury was painful, the wound missed Sasha's muscle. She recovered quickly and had mastered both the double axel and the triple salchow by October.

In 1997 Sasha was entering eighth grade and just a few weeks away from her thirteenth birthday when she stopped attending regular school. It was a big decision. Sasha and her parents decided she should switch to Futures High School. The school allows for flexible schedules so that youngsters can pursue a career and get a good education. Although she still had classes and homework, Sasha found it easier to juggle the demands of school and skating.

That fall, Sasha became a novice skater, just two ranks away from the highest level. Novice skaters compete at the national level, although they aren't up against the junior and senior skaters. Sasha was determined to skate at the 1998 Nationals, which would take place in Philadelphia, Pennsylvania. The event was especially exciting because 1998 was an Olympic year. The top three senior-level finishers would represent the

United States at the Games in Nagano, Japan. Sasha wanted to see the best in the United States skate at Senior Nationals.

Sasha came in second at Regionals as well as Sectionals. That qualified her for Nationals! But Sasha's performance at Nationals wasn't as strong. She stepped out of a combination during her short program. She was ranked in sixth place going into her long program. She struggled in her long program and ended up finishing sixth overall in the novice category.

Although it was a good showing for Sasha's first big competition, she was upset that she hadn't skated better. Sasha got over her disappointment quickly, however. She spent the rest of the week touring historic Philadelphia and watching the senior ladies vie for spots on the Olympic team. That year fifteen-year-old Tara Lipinski won silver and Michelle Kwan took the gold with a near-perfect performance.

One month later, Sasha watched Tara and Michelle on television at the Olympics in Nagano. This time Tara won gold and Michelle won silver. It was exciting having seen them skate at Nationals. Sasha felt closer to the action than ever before.

Sasha's pastimes off the ice include going to the movies, cooking, and designing skating outfits.

Sasha knew she was ready to become a junior. She took the test at the end of the 1997–1998 season and passed. Being a junior skater meant that Sasha needed to work on landing more triple jumps. So she spent the summer skating, picking out music for new programs, and designing costumes.

The 1998–1999 season started with a bang when Sasha won both junior Regionals and Sectionals, which took place in Arizona. The 1999 Nationals were in Salt Lake City. The city was already gearing up to host the 2002 Olympics. Sasha performed her long program on the same ice where the Olympic skaters would perform. She got a thrill imagining that she could be competing in the Olympics in just a few short years.

Perhaps she was busy imagining the future, but Sasha lost focus on the present at Nationals. She came in second after stepping out of one jump and two-footing another. Still, a silver medal was exciting. Sasha was even more thrilled to attend her first international event, the Val Gardena Winter Trophy competition in Ortisei, Italy. The northern Italian village was nestled in the Alps. Sasha won the event, and afterward she toured parts of Europe with her mother. They visited Germany, Switzerland, and Austria before returning to California.

Sasha also got the chance to perform with Champions on Ice. This ice show drew some of the biggest skating names during the off-season, including Michelle Kwan. It was awe-inspiring

26

for Sasha to be in the midst of world-class skaters, most of whom had Olympic and World medals. Performing for a crowd of twenty thousand at the Arrowhead Pond was also new for her. Sasha rose to the challenge and enjoyed the noncompetitive skating.

❝I'd like to cause a little riot in skating.❞

—SASHA COHEN

Before the 1999–2000 season began, Sasha passed the test to become a senior skater. She now had all the elements required to compete with the best in the world. Being with the best motivated Sasha to work even harder. She would compete against her old friend Naomi Narl Nam. For the first time ever, Sasha was more advanced than her competition. Her routines that year were more difficult than the other skaters' at Sectionals, and she easily won the gold.

The 2000 Nationals took place in Cleveland, Ohio. In her first big event as a senior, fifteen-year old Sasha was not expected to win a medal. The media described her as an up-and-coming skater. Everyone, including Sasha, was shocked when she was ranked first after her short program—ahead of both Naomi and Michelle! Sasha had skated exuberantly, unaware of her competitors' scores. "I was just so happy knowing I skated the best I could," Sasha later told one of the many reporters who wanted to talk to her.

THE GRAND PRIX

Part of the excitement of being a senior skater is the chance to compete at some of the Grand Prix events held each skating year. The Grand Prix takes place each fall. It begins with six competitions in six different countries. The skaters with the best scores from the initial competitions go on to the Grand Prix final. The Grand Prix also has junior-level events. Sasha won the Stockholm Trophy, held in Sweden, as a junior.

During the long program, Sasha was more aware of her standing and the media's new watchful eye. Her nerves got the better of her at the end, and she fell on her last jump, a triple toe loop. Sasha came in second to Michelle Kwan, who won her third Nationals. Although she was slightly disappointed, Sasha knew a silver-medal finish at her first senior Nationals was a big accomplishment. Suddenly, she was being considered a contender at the 2002 Olympics! All of the attention was flattering and a bit overwhelming.

Ordinarily, Sasha's second-place finish at Nationals would have meant that she qualified for the World Figure Skating

Championships, or Senior Worlds. However, the International Skating Union (ISU) had recently passed a rule stating that skaters who had not turned fifteen by July 1, 1999, could not compete at 2000 Senior Worlds. (Sasha had turned fifteen on October 26, 1999.) To get around the rule, Sasha needed to place in the top three at the World Junior Figure Skating Championships (also known as Junior Worlds), which were being held in Germany.

Figure-skating writer E. M. Swift was one of the first reporters to praise Sasha's abilities after the 2000 Nationals. He wrote: "[Sasha] moves her 4'9", seventy-nine-pound body about the ice as if she were a prima ballerina: assured, composed, impossibly flexible and elegant. . . . Her hands, her spirals, her posture, her positions in the air are flawless, breathtaking."

After her showing at Nationals, everyone assumed Sasha would finish in the top three at Junior Worlds. But Sasha soon learned to take nothing for granted. She missed some footwork during her short program and began to skate tentatively. After she missed her double axel, Sasha was in tears. But she believed she could still finish in the top three if she skated a clean long program.

Unfortunately for Sasha, it didn't work out that way. Although she skated a clean long program, she was not in the last group to skate. The top six finishers after the short program always skate in the final group. The judges typically hold their best marks for this last group of skaters since they're likely to skate the best. Sasha's heart sank as she watched the other skaters and realized that she would not be going to the World Championships. She ended up finishing sixth at Junior Worlds. Despite attending the party after the event, which was usually social Sasha's favorite part of competitions, Sasha couldn't cheer up. The hard worker was determined that the 2000–2001 season would be her best yet.

Chapter Four

Injuries and Training

Sasha resumed her intense training under even more intense media attention. She had never been interviewed except by local newspapers, but suddenly national magazines wanted to speak with her and TV shows were requesting interviews. Sasha attended the 2000 Teen Choice Awards and loved mingling with all of the celebrities. It was hard for her to believe that she was considered a sports celebrity. She didn't feel any different than she had before she'd won the silver medal at Nationals, but a lot had changed.

Sasha was expected to make a good showing at every event and medal as well. Her main competition was starting to change: Tara Lipinski had turned professional (making her ineligible to compete in Nationals or Worlds), and Michelle Kwan was attending college. Although Michelle was still skating, she was appearing at fewer competitions.

During the summer of 2000, Sasha trained at Ice Capades and Ice Castle as well as in Sun Valley, Idaho. One day while warming up, Sasha was stretching on the floor when her back cracked. What she didn't realize at the time was that she had injured herself. She remembered: "At first, it felt really good. But then I got up, and I couldn't step on my right foot at all. The pain was intense, and I didn't understand what had happened." Sasha couldn't bend forward or backward for the next week. She took it easy during practice, and the pain slowly went away. She quickly forgot about her back as the new skating season began.

❝ *I won't be the one standing in a corner just following along. I'm determined and stubborn.* ❞

—SASHA ON HERSELF

Sasha's first event of the season was a Grand Prix event called the Nations Cup. It took place in Germany. Sasha's skating was erratic, and she fell three times during her long program. But she picked herself up and got ready for her next competition.

The event was in Russia, a special place for Sasha's family. The entire Cohen family accompanied Sasha to the Cup of

Russia. This Grand Prix competition took place in St. Petersburg. Sasha was especially excited since it was her first trip to Russia. She skated cleanly and got standing ovations from the crowd, who knew her mother was from that part of the world. After she came in fourth place, a Russian newspaper awarded her a pretty hand-painted box. They said it was a prize for being the most beautiful skater at the event.

For her exhibition program at the Cup of Russia, Sasha accidentally gave the sound technician an uncut version of her program. It was five minutes long instead of four. She had to improvise a whole extra minute of skating!

Back home, Sasha noticed that the landings of her jumps were becoming more and more painful. Her back problem had returned. Both Sasha and Nicks were concerned. Over the next few weeks, doctors examined and x-rayed Sasha to try to figure out what was wrong. The doctors knew she was somehow injured, but they couldn't agree on what the injury was. (Doctors later determined that Sasha had extreme arthritis in a joint in her lower back.) Sasha continued training in between doctor visits.

The 2001 Nationals were being held in Boston, Massachusetts, and Sasha wanted to skate. Nicks didn't think it was a good idea, but Sasha won the argument, as she usually did with her coach. She desperately wanted to go to her first senior World Championships, and she needed to place in the top three finishers at Nationals to earn that honor. This Worlds was the last before the 2002 Olympics. Sasha felt strongly that she needed to skate at Worlds before she could be a contender at the Olympic Games.

Unfortunately, Sasha never got to skate at 2001 Nationals or Worlds. At a practice session in Boston, her jumps became so painful that she had to stop skating. Sasha finally realized that she couldn't compete at Nationals. She didn't take part in any competitions for the rest of the season. Doctors advised her to stop skating until her injury healed. Although she had to stop jumping on the ice, Sasha didn't stop training. She began physical therapy three times a week to strengthen her core muscles—the abdominal muscles and those surrounding the back.

When Sasha was injured, she used her time off to get her driver's license. She passed after taking driver's education classes with a friend.

Sasha noticed a difference in how she felt right away. She started training again, very carefully and slowly. By March 2001, she could try single jumps and modified versions of her routines. But she had another problem facing her—she needed a jump-free routine for the Champions on Ice tour and for a charity event that fellow skater Viktor Petrenko was hosting. Petrenko was born in Ukraine and had won the Olympic gold medal in 1992. He was raising money for the Children of Chernobyl Relief Fund.

The Chernobyl nuclear disaster occurred on April 26, 1986, when a nuclear reactor in Ukraine exploded. More than thirty people died instantly. Thousands more developed severe health problems. It is the world's worst nuclear disaster to date.

Sasha decided that if she couldn't wow the crowd with her jumps, she should use a prop to create interest. She created a ribbon program, and she learned how to twirl a ribbon around the ice and not get tangled up in it. This proved harder than she thought it would be. At the charity event, Sasha got tangled in the ribbon. She was embarrassed, especially after an audience member laughed.

Sasha's ego bounced back, though, and soon she was well on her way to recovery. By June she returned to her old training routine. She also began working on a new long program for the 2001–2002 skating season. Since she'd had to sit out much of the previous season, Sasha decided to stick with her old short program and focus all of her attention on a new long program.

Sasha wanted to skate to the music of the opera *Carmen,* by Georges Bizet. Nicks was against the idea. It wasn't the first time Sasha and her coach had clashed. He thought the music was too well known because both Katarina Witt and Debi Thomas had skated to *Carmen* in the 1988 Olympics. Despite the fact that fourteen years had passed, Nicks knew the skating world remembered it well.

Nicks changed his mind after hearing a discussion about Carmen's personality on the radio one day. "The deejay described Carmen as beautiful, tempestuous, flirtatious, confrontational, argumentative," he recalled. Nicks thought Carmen sounded a lot like Sasha. "I said, 'Sasha, it's a done deal.'" So Sasha got her way. She set to work choreographing the routine and helping design a costume.

Sasha's new routine was hard, and she was ready to rise to the challenge. But she needed help relearning some of her triple jumps. She hadn't been able to practice them in months. She wore a harnesslike device with a rope attached that allowed Nicks to stand nearby and hold an end like a fishing pole. As Sasha landed her jumps, Nicks would pull back with the rope. This allowed Sasha's landings to be gentler and less forceful on her healing back.

THE STORY OF CARMEN

The tragic opera *Carmen* is based on a short novel Prosper Mérimée wrote in the 1840s. It tells the story of a young soldier named Don José, who falls for a beautiful and headstrong Spanish factory worker named Carmen. He rescues Carmen from prison after she is involved in a fight. Don José himself serves a prison sentence for helping Carmen escape, and Carmen tries to convince him to run away with her. When he refuses, the tempestuous Carmen falls for a bullfighter named Escamillo. In a jealous rage, Don José murders Carmen.

After she regained her confidence, Sasha used the harness to work on landing a quadruple salchow. This jump starts off on a back inside edge, has four revolutions in the air, and ends on the back outside edge of the other foot. Very few female skaters attempted any quadruple jump. If she landed the jump in competition, Sasha would become the first female skater ever to do so. "It's something to give me an edge over my competition and a chance to make history," Sasha said.

Although she landed the jump in practice, Sasha wasn't as lucky her first time trying it in competition. When she attempted it at the Finlandia Trophy in Helsinki, Finland, she fell on the landing. But Sasha still won the event.

SEPTEMBER 11, 2001

Like most Americans, Sasha will never forget where she was on the day of the World Trade Center attacks. She had returned from the Goodwill Games in Australia the day before and was sleeping in when her mom woke her up to watch the tragic news.

At the Skate America competition in the fall of 2001, Sasha landed several quads at a practice session that ABC television was filming. Finally, she had concrete evidence that she could land the quad. The crowd watching was thrilled, as were her fellow skaters. "I was just blown away," said Timothy Goebel, the first person to land a quadruple salchow in competition. "Some of her landings were as nice as any I've landed in competition. I was really amazed." Sasha still loves to watch the tape and recall how amazing it felt to nail the landing.

Unfortunately, she was left wondering how it would feel to land the quad in an actual competition. Sasha tried the jump at

Skate America, but she got nervous right before the takeoff. She ended up doing only a single salchow. Her concentration was shot, and Sasha never recovered her composure. She later described the long program at 2001 Skate America as one of the worst of her life.

Sasha was determined to put the competition behind her to prepare for the 2002 Nationals, which would determine the Olympic team. Nationals took place in Los Angeles, and Sasha was happy to have her family nearby. She was nervous about having missed the previous Nationals. All the pressure made it an easy decision to cut the quad from her routine in favor of two easier jumps. "I don't think I need to prove myself," Sasha told reporters before Nationals. "I have had some good skates and bad skates. I'm going out to get a spot on the team and not necessarily to prove myself."

Sasha got a second cat, a tiny white kitten named Mia, around Christmas 2001. Sasha snuck Mia into the hotel to stay with her at the 2002 Nationals.

Twenty-one-year-old Michelle Kwan was considered a lock for a spot on the team, as was sixteen-year-old skating sensation Sarah Hughes. The third spot on the team was a toss-up between Sasha and twenty-one-year-old Angela Nikodinov.

After Sasha's short program, it looked as if the third spot might belong to her. She skated a clean program to a waltz and came in second behind Michelle. Sarah was in third place and Angela in fourth. "[Sasha] skated with verve and nerve. She showed off flexibility she learned as a gymnast with a series of spirals," wrote a reporter. But Sasha knew her biggest challenge—the long program—was yet to come.

Two days later, nerves and suspense were mounting as the final group of skaters took the ice to warm up before the long program. In that time, Sasha and Michelle bumped into each other twice. Some thought the collision was intentional on Sasha's part, but she said it was an accident.

❝The warm-up is only six minutes, and we are all trying to get all our elements in. No one is going to get out of the way for anyone else. It's very intense out there. Most people realize there are a lot of close calls.**❞**

—SASHA AFTER BUMPING INTO MICHELLE KWAN DURING THE WARM-UP FOR THE LONG PROGRAM AT THE 2002 NATIONALS

After the warm-up, Sasha went behind the curtain, took off her skates, and lay on the floor to try to calm down and prepare for the most important skate of her life so far. The performance turned out to be one of Sasha's most memorable.

She landed six triples and even added a seventh, which she put her hand down on. But it didn't matter because Sasha's other jumps were clean, and her spins and spirals were exceptional. Sasha later said, *"Carmen* inspired me, and I skated passionately. It earned me second place, with Michelle in first and Sarah in third. I couldn't stop smiling, couldn't stop thinking . . . *I made the Olympic team!"* After her exuberant long program and silver-medal win, no one questioned that Sasha had earned her place on the U.S. Olympic team.

Chapter | Five

First Olympics

Sasha had only a few short weeks before she left for Salt Lake City—and she had a lot to do. Instead of returning to train at their regular rink, Sasha and Nicks headed to Lake Arrowhead for more free ice time and fewer distractions.

Sasha did make time for a once-in-a-lifetime opportunity to carry the Olympic torch near her grandparents' home in San Diego. The Olympic torch relay is an important event, and before Nationals, Sasha had enthusiastically agreed to be part of it. She was doubly excited to carry it knowing that she was going to be competing in the Games herself.

When Sasha boarded the plane to Salt Lake City, she felt very aware of how monumental the next several weeks could be. She was hoping for a medal but not expecting it. The competition awaiting her was fierce. Michelle Kwan was a crowd favorite, and many felt she had deserved the gold in Nagano in

1998. At age twenty-one, she was one of the older skaters in the group. Sasha's other teammate, Sarah Hughes, was one of the younger competitors. She was one year younger than Sasha and relatively new to the senior skating scene. She had made an impressive showing in the events she had competed in so far. She had even come in third at the 2001 Worlds (which Sasha had missed). Russian skater Irina Slutskaya, known for her athleticism and complex jump combinations, was the biggest threat to the U.S. team. Many reporters and skating commentators considered the U.S. women's figure-skating team to be the strongest in a decade. Some even believed they could sweep the medals podium (take the gold, silver, and bronze medals).

Before skating could begin, however, Sasha had to settle into the Olympic Village that had been created on the campus of the University of Utah. She was given so much Olympic clothing and supplies that she had a hard time fitting everything into the tiny dormitory room she shared with Sarah Hughes, ice dancer Naomi Lang, and pairs skater Kyoko Ina.

A day later, the Olympic teams from every country marched in the opening ceremonies to officially start the 2002 Winter Games. The march was long (three miles) and cold. Luckily, Sasha had prepared by bundling up in lots of layers. The march turned out to be more exciting than Sasha expected.

"That was one of the most incredible moments in the entire Olympic experience for me—turning the corner and walking inside [the stadium]," she recalled. "It was breathtaking."

For Sasha's opening ceremony walk, she stayed warm by wearing long underwear, fleece pants, a couple of thermals, two turtlenecks, a sweater, a scarf, two pairs of gloves, two pairs of socks, and a pair of sheepskin boots.

What happened next was even more amazing. Sasha discovered that the empty seat next to her was reserved for the president of the United States! Sasha used her cell phone to call her mom and put the president on the line to chat with Galina. "I want you to know not to worry," President Bush assured Galina. "Your daughter is behaving very well."

As much as Sasha wanted to stay at the Olympic Village and socialize with the other athletes, the environment was too distracting. With almost two weeks between opening ceremonies and the start of the ladies' competition, she decided to fly back to Lake Arrowhead for more training. When Sasha returned to Salt Lake City, she and Galina checked into a hotel. They tried to stay away from the bustle of the Village as much as possible.

66 *[In 1998] Tara really did attack out there where you could say Michelle did hold back out there. I guess I would say I don't hold back. People are expecting Irina [Slutskaya] and Michelle to be in those two spots. Hopefully, the door will open for someone else. If it does, I'll be ready.* 99

— SASHA ON THE 1998 OLYMPICS OUTCOME
AND HER CHANCES AT THE 2002 GAMES

The night of the short program, Sasha tried to forget about winning and focus on skating a clean routine, one element at a time. She took the ice in a sparkly costume of different shades of blue, ready to skate to waltz music from the Russian film *My Sweet and Tender Beast*. Suddenly, her nervousness disappeared. "All the nerves happen off the ice for me," Sasha explained. "Once they called my name, no butterflies. I just felt this calm, and I just went out there to attack."

After landing her first combination jump, a triple lutz–double toe, Sasha's confidence soared. Smiling, she relaxed and hit all eight of the required elements with ease and enthusiasm. As her music ended, the crowd was on its feet, throwing bunches of flowers down to the ice. Sasha had skated a clean program. She received excellent marks and was in first place for a short time.

❝ Whenever I'm in a competition, I always want to be on top of the podium. I've been working really hard for Salt Lake and, hopefully, I can be on the top of the podium.❞

—SASHA COHEN

Michelle and Irina skated after Sasha, and both placed above her. But at the end of the night, Sasha was still in third place. Sarah was in fourth place. That meant Sasha was definitely in contention for a medal. "I was just so happy I got the marks I deserved," Sasha later told reporters. "I just want to keep it together [for the long program]."

With one day off between the short and long program, Sasha relaxed and tried to sleep as much as she could. But it was hard to unwind when she was on such a high from her short program performance. She ran through each element of the long program in her mind as she tried to fall asleep. On the morning of the competition, Sasha went to practice her jumps at the rink. All seemed well until she tried her triple lutz and kept falling. Something was wrong. Her timing was off. Sasha was scared she wouldn't get the jump back before that night. Determined not to let the lutz ruin her performance, Sasha and Galina tracked down a videotape of Nationals. Seeing herself do the jump correctly helped Sasha get her timing back in her head, but she was still nervous.

THE ODD COUPLE

Sasha's relationship with John Nicks is full of difference and debate. Sasha is known for not giving up or giving in. "It's not that I don't want to follow his instructions," Sasha explained. "It's just that I have my own ideas. I like to push people and I like to push myself." *International Figure Skating* magazine called the duo "The Odd Couple." And even Nicks can't explain the relationship. "It's absolutely abnormal," he said. "I've coached over a thousand skaters in the last forty years and I've never had anything like this. It's most interesting and most challenging."

Arriving at the rink that night, Sasha unpacked her skating bag only to discover that she had misplaced her tights. She had ten minutes to find another pair before the warm-up. Luckily, another skater who had already performed loaned Sasha her tights. Sasha made it out onto the ice for the warm-up for the final group of six skaters. The six had drawn numbers to determine the order in which they would skate that night. Sarah was skating second, Sasha fourth, Michelle fifth, and Irina was set to skate last. "That's good for Sasha," said Richard Callaghan, Tara Lipinski's former coach. "She's going to skate the standard that the other girls have to skate up to. They can do it, but it won't be easy."

In the warm-up, Sasha tried out the triple lutz that had given her such trouble that morning. She had the jump back. She also cleanly landed her triple-triple combinations. She was as ready as she could be. She watched as Sarah Hughes skated a clean long program that had the crowd on its feet. It was a great performance, but the top three skaters still had to perform.

Sasha skated out onto the rink and struck her opening pose as Carmen. "This is what I've been preparing for, what I've been working so hard for," she told herself. "I'm ready." Seconds into the program, she nailed her first jump—the double axel. Her next jump, forty-five seconds into the program, was a combination triple lutz–triple toe loop. Sasha landed the lutz but fell on the triple toe. She was stunned but determined to get through the remaining three minutes of her program. Despite her shock, Sasha managed to skate the rest of the program without any mistakes, but she later admitted that her heart just wasn't in the routine. When her marks were lower than Sarah's, Sasha knew that she wouldn't be winning a medal at the Olympics.

Sasha had a hard time caring about what happened after her own routine, but Michelle and Irina were still left to skate. They both struggled with their triple-triple combinations as well. Sarah, who had skated as if she didn't have a care in the world or a chance to win a medal, suddenly found herself with an Olympic gold medal. It was an unusual and surprising twist to the most anticipated and talked-about women's event in years. Irina took home the silver medal and Michelle won the bronze. Sasha came in fourth place. On the bright side, she had been to the Olympics and planned to be back again in four years.

---

66 *Millions of little girls around the country have dreams of winning an Olympic gold medal, and that's my dream as well.* **99**

—SASHA COHEN

Sasha skated well the next night at the exhibition in which the top skaters performed. Afterward, she finally had a chance to explore the Olympic Village. She even attended the gold medal hockey game, which was especially exciting because the U.S. team was playing Canada. (Canada won 5–2.) Sasha also attended a big party *Sports Illustrated* magazine threw for all the athletes. Then she returned home to California.

Although the Olympics were over, the skating year was not. The World Championships were being held in Nagano, Japan. It was Sasha's first time competing in the event. She was excited to finally be there and anxious to get more international experience. Many reporters had speculated that Sasha's inexperience in big international events had been one of her biggest weaknesses at the Games.

Unfortunately, just like the Olympics, Sasha's first World Championships didn't go as she had hoped. The day before her short program, Sasha decided to go for a jog. Even though she was in great shape, Sasha wasn't used to this sort of training. After she jogged for almost an hour, Sasha knew it had been a mistake. Her legs were shot. Nicks had no advice. He only hoped she would have time to recover. During her routine, Sasha stepped out of her double axel. She then fell twice in her long program. Again she finished in fourth, just out of medal contention.

Sasha was tired from a long season. She knew she needed a vacation before she could start planning for the 2002–2003 season. The Cohen family, along with Sasha's friend Tiffany Stiegler, traveled to Hawaii. The weather was warm and sunny, and Sasha went to the beach and relaxed. The trip was just what she needed.

Sasha had another reason to pamper herself. Just weeks after returning home, she had graduated from high school with straight As. She would no longer have to juggle schoolwork with skating. Although she decided not to attend college immediately, Sasha has said she may go back to school in the future.

For her senior year of high school, Sasha had decided to return to a regular school. She enrolled part-time at local Aliso Niguel High School. Her favorite class was economics. Her favorite school activities were hanging out with her friends and attending dances.

That summer Sasha decided to perform with Champions on Ice again. The tour included forty-four shows, which were fun but exhausting as well. The group sometimes performed two shows in one day. When they weren't skating, they were on the tour bus getting to the next destination. "Sometimes it just felt like we were sleeping, driving, and skating!" Sasha said.

Vacationing in Hawaii and traveling with Champions on Ice would have kept her busy all summer, but in July 2002, she traveled to Great Britain as well. She had been asked to perform at the Golden Jubilee to celebrate the fifty-year reign of Queen Elizabeth II. Sasha couldn't pass up this once-in-a-lifetime opportunity. The event was hosted by Olympic ice dancers Jayne Torvill and Christopher Dean. It also included fellow U.S. skater

Kristi Yamaguchi, who won gold in the 1992 Olympics. Sasha was thrilled to finally meet Kristi, who was one of her skating idols, and perform her ribbon routine for the queen. She even got to shake the queen's hand afterward.

Even with all the travel she was doing, Sasha still had to create new routines and train for the next season. A Russian coach named Nikolai Morozov, who worked with famed coach Tatiana Tarasova, came to Lake Arrowhead to help create Sasha's new programs. After her British performance, Sasha flew to Connecticut to finish her work with Morozov. There Sasha met Tarasova.

Tarasova had worked with some of the biggest names in skating, including Olympic gold medalists Ilia Kulik and Alexei Yagudin. Sasha was thrilled to receive individual instruction from the legendary coach. She was also amazed at how much ice time she was allowed. The rink was often empty, and she and Tarasova were usually alone on the ice. After the crowded rinks in Southern California and only forty-five minutes a day of coaching from Nicks (who coached many skaters beside Sasha), Sasha began to think about moving to Connecticut. She was out of high school and about to turn eighteen. Many of her friends were already on their own.

She discussed the move with her mom, who agreed that it made sense considering where Sasha was in her career. But

Galina wanted to make the move as a family. Natasha was about to start high school, and Roger could continue working as a lawyer from just about anywhere. It seemed like the right time for a big change. Switching coasts was a lot of work for the family. Packing up a house after living there almost ten years was time-consuming. Leaving friends and grandparents was difficult as well. But by Labor Day, the Cohen family had relocated from Laguna Niguel, California, to Avon, Connecticut.

Chapter Six

A New Coach, a New Coast

Sasha's move to the East Coast and switch to Tarasova stunned the skating world and shocked Nicks. Tarasova was known for giving skaters with good jumping skills more polish and presentation in their routines. Sasha, however, was already known for her lyricism on the ice. Her flexibility and extensions often drew comparisons to a ballet dancer. "I think that what Sasha needs most is consistency and advanced jumping work," Nicks said.

Sasha was getting more intense training and individual attention. Those seemed to be paying off with her new routines, a short program to "Malagueña" by Ernesto Lecuona and long program set to music from a piano concerto by Sergei Rachmaninoff. Sasha loved her new programs for the 2002–2003 season.

The first season after an Olympic year is like having a clean slate—the start of a four-year cycle full of promise and excitement. Sports journalist Christine Brennan wrote an article about Sasha early in the season. "To call the eighteen-year-old Cohen a disappointment is the raw truth," she said, "but it's also too definitive a description because she is not yet finished. To call her tantalizing is more like it, because she has been exactly that, so close to greatness, yet never quite there."

Determined that this be her year of opportunity, Sasha headed to Daytona Beach, Florida, for the Campbell's Classic. Sasha placed just off the medals podium in fourth place. But she was happy with the way she had skated. Since it was only October, she was also optimistic that she would improve as the skating season wore on. And she was even more excited about her next skating opportunity. She had been asked to open the rink at Rockefeller Center in New York City. It was nice not to have to compete and just enjoy her surroundings—tall skyscrapers and open sky.

❝I've never lived in a place that changes seasons, and it's so gorgeous.**❞**

—SASHA ON LIVING IN CONNECTICUT

Soon enough, however, it was back to competition. Skate Canada in November 2002 was the first big event of the season. Sasha took home the gold medal. She then went on to dazzle at the Trophée Lalique, also in November. She came in first and won a glass medal as well as a crystal trophy. Next up was Sasha's final Grand Prix event, the Cup of Russia, which took place in Moscow, Russia, in late November. Coming off two previous wins, Sasha was on a high, and her skating showed off her good mood. She landed six triple jumps but still came in second to Russian Victoria Volchkova.

In 2002 Sasha rode on a float in the Macy's Thanksgiving Day parade in New York City. Despite the freezing weather, Sasha had a lot of fun!

Sasha's next event was the Sears Figure Skating Open. She performed a brand-new artistic program to *Romeo and Juliet.* Again her skating was near flawless. She even got her first perfect score from the judges. After all of her skating disappointments, getting her first 6.0 was a wonderful feeling. Almost as good was her showing at the next event, the International Figure Skating Challenge in mid-December. Once again, Sasha landed six triple jumps. Even though she stepped out of a seventh, she took home the gold medal again.

The holidays were a favorite time for Sasha and the Cohen family, who experienced their first New England winter. The snow was fun at first, but Sasha wasn't used to the cold. She didn't mind leaving Connecticut in January 2003 to head to the warmer climate of Dallas, Texas, for the U.S. Figure Skating Championships.

The media was buzzing that this was Sasha's year. She had been on a roll, winning two out of her last three competitions. Heading into the 2003 Nationals, she was even favored to win. Sasha wasn't as sure as the skating experts, but she was flattered by the attention. "It's just as strong a field as an Olympic year. I feel I've become a stronger competitor this year. . . . Quite a few girls could win the title. . . . I'd definitely like to win," Sasha said.

Nationals was the first competition of the season at which all three of the top U.S. ladies would skate. Sarah Hughes had sat out several events with a torn muscle behind her knee, and Michelle Kwan had skated in events that Sasha had missed. Finally, all three were in the same place for the first time since the 2002 Olympics. Sasha felt ready to show everyone, including herself, that she could keep it together through both a short and a long program. "The long program is a very hard program for most skaters and something that I definitely still need more work on. But I feel like I'm getting there," Sasha said.

The short program was a fairly good start for Sasha. She made a small error on the landing of her combination jump and was in second place heading into the all-important long program. She was determined to skate a clean long.

> ❝ *There's always an advantage in competing more times, getting your programs out there and just getting comfortable with them under pressure in competition. But my competitors are very strong. The U.S. ladies are the strongest in the world. So Nationals will be a tough competition.* ❞
>
> —SASHA COHEN

In the long program, Sasha began by two-footing her triple-triple combination. But then she landed three triples without a wobble. With all of her difficult elements behind her, Sasha was just starting to relax when she suddenly changed her routine. Instead of going for her planned combination jump, she tried for a triple toe loop. She hesitated and fell hard on the ice. The audience let out a gasp.

Sasha had to pick herself up and continue with her program. But she was so disappointed that the tears starting flowing before she even left the ice. Even though she came in third and won the bronze medal, Sasha couldn't believe she had blown it again. "I'd put too much pressure on myself," she explained. "I didn't go with it. You have to trust your body, you can't hesitate or question yourself. I'd let my mind wander, and it ruined my performance."

Fifteen-year-old Sasha Cohen learns that she's won the silver medal at the 2000 U.S. Figure Skating Championships in Cleveland, Ohio.

© Brian Bahr/Allsport/Getty Images

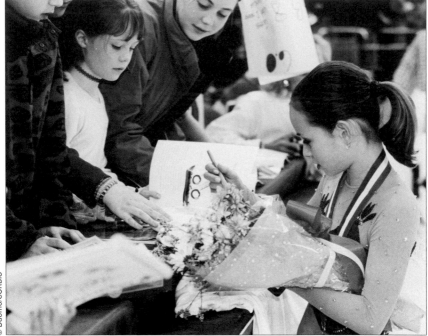

© Duomo/CORBIS

Sasha signs autographs for fans at the 2000 U.S. Figure Skating Championships.

© Al Bello/Getty Images

Sasha performs a layback spin during her short program at the 2002 Winter Olympic Games in Salt Lake City, Utah. In her first Olympic appearance, Sasha finished in fourth place.

Sasha *(center front)* poses with skaters at the 2002 Disney Ice Summer Camp in Anaheim, California. Sasha grew up in California. The warm state produces a significant number of top figure skaters.

© Shelly Castellano/Icon SMI

© Fernando Salas/ZUMA Press

Sasha *(right)* and her younger sister, Natasha, have always been close. Here they attend a 2003 fashion show in New York City.

Sasha practices before the 2006 U.S. Figure Skating Championships in St. Louis, Missouri. This spiral position shows off her incredible flexibility.

© Matthew Stockman/Getty Images

© Steve Boyle/NewSport/CORBIS

Sasha and her coach, John Nicks, react to her high marks after her long program at the 2006 U.S. Figure Skating Championships. Sasha finished this competition in first place.

© Robert Laberge/Getty Images

At the 2006 Winter Olympic Games, Sasha won a silver medal. She poses with gold medalist Shizuka Arakawa of Japan *(center)* and bronze medalist Irina Slutskaya of Russia *(right)*.

© Frazer Harrison/Getty Images

Sasha took time off from skating in 2006–2007 to pursue an acting career. In spring 2007, she attended the premiere of the figure skating comedy *Blades of Glory*.

Sasha needed some time off to get over Nationals. To get her mind off things, she traveled to California to visit her friends and stop by her old rink. She did some modeling. After the Olympics, Sasha had signed on with the renowned William Morris Agency. She had received so many offers to make appearances and endorse products that having a manager and agent became a necessity. In early 2003, she did a fashion shoot for *Seventeen* magazine, as well as a photo shoot and commercial for an endorsement deal with Citizen Watch.

All of the distraction was good for Sasha, but it was soon time to return to skating. The Grand Prix Final was being held from February 28 to March 2 in St. Petersburg, Russia. Sasha, Tatiana, and Galina first flew to Paris, France, for the week before the event. They were soon joined by Roger and Natasha as well as Sasha's grandparents. Having her family there made her time in Paris feel more like a vacation than preparation for a big competition. Sasha trained each day and toured the city, taking in the sights, shopping, and eating at some of the city's best restaurants.

The relaxation was just what Sasha needed before competing again. She was the only U.S. skater at the event. She wanted to perform as well as she could, not only for herself but for her country. Russian Irina Slutskaya was the fan favorite, and the ladies competition came down to Irina and Sasha. Neither skater was perfect in her long program. Sasha made one mistake but hit all of her jumps and received first-place marks from all the judges. She was the first American to win a Grand Prix final since 1998. Even more important, Sasha got her confidence back on the ice.

Sasha hardly had time to catch her breath before the 2003 World Championships, which were being held in Washington, D.C. She was determined not to let the pressure, regret, and her own overanalyzing get in the way of her skating anymore. "Every time you don't skate perfectly, there's always something to regret," Sasha said. "That's something I'm working on eliminating. I would love to get a world title, but that's not what I'm focusing on. I'm focusing on each element, one by one."

Still, Sasha wanted to win at Worlds. Her first challenge was the qualifying round, which was worth 20 percent of the total score. Skaters perform their long programs to qualify. The top thirty skaters from this round go on to compete in the short program. Sasha skated a clean program to qualify, so her chances were looking good. Disaster struck in the short program, however, when she fell on her triple flip. She finished the short program in fourth place, which meant that even if she skated a perfect long program, she couldn't win gold.

Sasha lost her concentration in the long program and shocked the audience when she fell in the middle of a spin. Later, she fell on the landing of a triple toe loop. Sasha ended the competition in fourth place, behind first-place Michelle Kwan, second-place Elena Sokolova of Russia, and third-place Fumie Suguri of Japan. The season was over. While it had started well for Sasha, it didn't end the way she had wanted it to end. She was looking forward to summer and another Champions on Ice tour before the next skating season began.

THE TRIPLE FLIP

In a flip jump, a skater pushes off the back inside edge of the skate while digging the toe pick of the opposite foot into the ice. After completing the desired number of revolutions in the air, the skater lands on the picking foot. No female skater landed a triple flip in competition until the 1981 European Championships. At that event, both Katarina Witt of East Germany and Manuela Ruben of West Germany landed triple flips.

Sasha focused on getting into great shape both physically and mentally. She started eating more healthful foods, working out regularly, and taking good care of herself. That summer, she skated better and more consistently than she ever had on tour. While she had once needed a warm-up before performing,

Sasha could now step onto the ice and hit all of her elements in her exhibition program. She had never felt more powerful on the ice.

❝Tatiana is the first person that's expected more out of myself than I've expected out of myself. I always set huge and very lofty goals for myself.❞

—SASHA COHEN

Before the hectic season began, Sasha decided to take a vacation—this time without her family. She and her friend Christie Baca traveled to Cancún, Mexico, to soak up the sun and swim. It was the first time Sasha had ever been on vacation without her mother. In 2003, at almost nineteen years old, Sasha knew she was ready to take this important step. Galina had no reason to worry about her daughter. Sasha was never the type to get into trouble. She and Christie preferred to hang out by the pool and eat limes!

But Sasha didn't maintain a balanced diet in Mexico. Sasha usually ate well, but she had so much else to do on vacation that she lost four pounds. At 5'2" and only ninety-five pounds, that much weight loss was significant. Tatiana was determined to get her student back in shape. Sasha resumed her training and was soon back to normal thanks to a healthful diet, weight training, running, and on-ice training.

With Sasha stronger than ever, all that was left before the 2003–2004 season got under way was some new programs. Sasha decided to keep her short program to "Malagueña" and use music from the ballet *Swan Lake* for her new long. Although the music was popular in the skating world, just as *Carmen* was, Tatiana had selected some less familiar parts of the music. Her selections gave the music a new twist. Although they agreed that the music was a good choice, Tatiana and Sasha disagreed over the costume. Tatiana wanted Sasha decked out in feathers like a swan, while Sasha didn't want a feather on her costume. The two compromised, and soon the slightly feathered costume—and Sasha—were ready for the new season.

Chapter Seven

Coming Together

Sasha had a packed schedule for the 2003–2004 season, but she was ready for it. She felt stronger and more relaxed and centered than she had ever been. Her first event was the Campbell's Classic Invitational at Madison Square Garden in New York City. Sasha wasn't prepared for the audience's reaction to her performance. After hitting each element and skating with ease, she got a standing ovation! She won the competition, beating Michelle Kwan for the first time. "It was quite a way to start a season," Sasha remembered.

Skate America was next, and Sasha was excited. The exhibition skate for the event was scheduled for October 26, her nineteenth birthday. Sasha got an early birthday present when she won the event and again received standing ovations after both her short and long programs. She celebrated her birthday by taking a limousine into New York City, where she spent her time eating and shopping. A couple of days later, she had an appearance on the *Today Show*. The media was speculating that this was Sasha's year, and she was feeling confident as well.

Skate Canada only boosted Sasha's confidence. Once again, she won and was ready for the next challenge: Trophée Lalique in France. Sasha loved her crystal trophy from the last season and wanted another to make a pair. After skating a clean short program, she was halfway there. But then Sasha started to feel sick. It was flu season, and all of Sasha's traveling was leaving her feeling run-down. She stayed in bed the next day instead of practicing and did only a light warm-up the day of the long program. Although she put her hand down on a double axel, Sasha was happy with her performance. So were the judges. Sasha won her fourth-straight event.

Sasha's key to surviving New England winters? Lots of layers! She bought turtlenecks, long underwear, sweaters, coats, and boots to keep warm.

The flu was slowing her down, but Sasha couldn't give in to it completely. She had agreed to skate at a cancer fund-raiser that fellow skater Scott Hamilton had organized in Cleveland, Ohio. Sasha was determined to be there. Afterward, she met her family in Miami, Florida, for a few days' rest. Sasha hoped to recharge so she'd be ready for her December competitions and the upcoming holiday season.

SCOTT HAMILTON

Scott Hamilton is considered one of the greatest male figure skaters of all time. The four-time World champion and 1984 Olympic gold medalist turned professional and cofounded the skating tour Stars on Ice. He skated in and produced the show for fifteen years while battling both testicular cancer and a benign brain tumor. Now cancer free, Scott is married with a son and is a popular TV skating commentator.

Her sickness behind her, Sasha's next event was the International Skating Challenge in Auburn Hills, Michigan, in early December. Although she was feeling better, Sasha's skating took a turn for the worse at the competition. She fell three times and stepped out of a jump during her long program. Besides the shock of falling, Sasha was all wet from landing in a puddle on the ice. After placing third, Sasha just wanted to go home. Unfortunately, a big snowstorm had hit the East Coast, and Galina and Sasha got stuck in Washington, D.C. Because all flights were grounded, they took a very long train ride home.

Sasha's perfect season had come to an end. It only got worse at the Grand Prix Final on December 12 and 13 in Colorado Springs, Colorado. The higher altitude was hard on Sasha, as it is on many athletes. There is less oxygen at the high mountain elevations, and it is often harder to breathe, especially while exercising. In addition, Sasha's back had begun acting up a little. To make things worse, Tatiana wasn't well— nor was Tatiana's mother back in Russia. All of these things added up to trouble on the ice for Sasha. She fell once during her short program on a triple lutz and twice during the long program—on a triple toe and a flip. All told, she had fallen six times in her last eleven minutes on the ice. Despite all of her mistakes, Sasha came in second at the competition.

Sasha had several weeks off before the 2004 Nationals, but she felt she needed to do more than just rest. She needed to make some changes if she was going to finish the season strong. She decided it was time for a new coach. Tatiana needed time to tend to her health problems, and she and Sasha weren't connecting on the ice as they once had. The pair decided to part ways. "I am grateful for everything Tatiana has done for me, both personally and for my skating," Sasha said in a statement. "I wish her all the best, and I hope she has a speedy recovery."

66 *Lately I have not been feeling well. The amount of travel to Sasha's international competitions has adversely affected my health. Physically, I need to have a less rigorous schedule. I will be going back to Russia to take care of myself. I wish Sasha all the best in the future.* **99**

—Tatiana Tarasova on parting with Sasha

Just days after the disastrous Grand Prix, Roger contacted Robin Wagner, who had coached Sarah Hughes to her Olympic gold medal in Salt Lake. Sarah was a full-time student at Yale University that year, so Wagner hadn't been coaching. She was vacationing in Florida when she got a message from the Cohens. They met for dinner, and the Cohens soon revealed that they wanted Robin to be Sasha's new coach. Robin was more than enthusiastic. She recalled: "I excused myself to the ladies' room and I walked outside and went 'YESSS!' I came back in, sat down, and said very coolly, 'OK, when would you like to get started?'"

The answer to Wagner's question was "immediately." Nationals were only two weeks away. After the 2003 Nationals, Sasha was anxious to skate well. So, just two days before Christmas, they started to train. The pressure was on, but the two got along well from the start. Robin was out on the ice, skating beside Sasha, showing her what to do instead of just telling her. Although Sasha was a confident skater, Robin wanted Sasha to be more aggressive on the ice and attack her routines. "It's not in her nature [to be aggressive]," Robin explained. "I think very often you'll hear many of the skaters say they tend to pull back a little bit. It's a lot easier to pull back than to push forward. . . . That's why I push so hard for her to skate at the ultimate level."

> **❝**I am absolutely thrilled I was asked and to have the opportunity to work with Sasha. She is a wonderful talent. . . . It's going to be a great challenge to help her realize her potential. It is a luxury for me to work with someone such as Sasha who can become a real standout in the history of our sport.**❞**
>
> —ROBIN WAGNER ON WORKING WITH SASHA

Sasha felt as though Robin's pushing was paying off. They trained hard every day for two weeks. Robin drove three hours each way from her home on Long Island, New York (east of New York City), to the rink. The arrangement was exhausting but necessary since Robin wanted Sasha focused on her training instead of on traveling.

The holidays, always busy for Sasha with family celebrations and preparations for Nationals, were especially hectic with a new coach. Still, Sasha baked and ate a lot. Galina made her delicious truffles, and Sasha gave homemade cookies to everyone at the rink. Sasha's grandparents and great-aunt and great-uncle flew in from California, and the Cohen family enjoyed their time together.

All too soon, it was time to leave for Nationals in Atlanta, Georgia. Sasha felt as rested and prepared as possible. Robin's coaching had improved her confidence. "Robin has brought a little more fun and joy to skating and at the same time she pushes me just as hard," Sasha said before Nationals. Robin and Sasha checked into a different hotel than the other skaters to try to avoid both the media and other distractions as they got ready for the competition.

Sasha shone in her short program to "Malagueña." And she was in first place at the end of the evening, ahead of Michelle Kwan. Two days later, she was skating first in the last batch of six skaters in the long program. Sasha had a five-minute warm-up before her four-minute routine. As she took the ice, Sasha realized that she had overdone it during the warm-up. By the middle of her routine, she was exhausted. Sasha missed her triple toe loop, a jump she never missed in practice. She didn't give up, however, and she finished the routine strong. Sasha won the silver but refused to be disappointed. Robin was keeping her motivated for Worlds in a couple of months. Thanks to her positive attitude, Sasha skated a beautiful exhibition program to close the competition.

When Sasha wasn't training, a favorite activity of hers was going into New York City and exploring. She had always loved New York and was getting to know the city and all it had to offer. The shopping and dining were incredible. Sasha was determined to try as many new restaurants (and as many new desserts) as possible.

Sasha fell into a comfortable routine in January and February 2004. On days she trained, she warmed up and skated for an hour and a half in the morning before taking an hour-and-a-half break during which she ate lunch and rested. In the afternoon, she hit the ice for another hour and a half of skating. After, she did Pilates (a form of conditioning that uses controlled movements to strengthen and tone the body), office training, or physical therapy. She and Robin were working on stroking (pushing off on one foot) and triple-triple jump combinations. They also started working on an exhibition program, set to music from *My Fair Lady,* Sasha's favorite movie. She loved playing Eliza Doolittle (the movie's main character). She began the program wearing an overcoat and hat and then removed them to reveal a beautiful dress. Sasha was excited to skate the program for exhibition numbers and the upcoming spring Champions on Ice tour.

By mid-February 2004, the Cohen family had decided to look for an apartment on New York City's Upper West Side. Until they had a home in the city, Sasha decided to stay during the week with Robin at her home on Long Island. Robin gave Sasha the entire second floor to call home. Sasha had her own bedroom and television. It was much easier to keep her focus and commute from Robin's home.

Sasha liked to cook at the Wagner house for Robin and her husband, Jerry. Before Sasha moved in, the couple hardly used their kitchen. Sasha enjoyed making breakfasts, such as oatmeal, and lots of delicious, healthful dinners.

With Worlds just weeks away, the duo was working harder than ever. Despite Sasha's place among the world's most elite skaters, they had found areas that needed some improvement. Robin and Sasha focused on Sasha's edge work, combination jumps, and overall polish.

Sasha, Robin, and Galina left for Worlds, which were being held in Dortmund, Germany, a few days early so Sasha could get used to the time difference. She stayed up during the day and ate meals at the new time so that within two days, she was accustomed to her schedule. Sasha realized that part of the reason she usually fell in the long programs was that she was tired. Her short was generally clean, but by the long, she often felt exhausted. She was determined to pace herself and not burn out.

❝*I have to focus on one element at a time and not be overwhelmed by the whole program. I can't keep thinking back to something else in the program and say, 'Oh, I wish I could do that again.' . . . I can't think that way. I'd rather look at what I've done.*❞

—SASHA COHEN

First up was the qualifying round. Everyone expected Sasha to breeze through qualifying, but she had learned not to take anything for granted. The Wednesday qualifier was worth 20 percent of the final score, the short program on Friday was worth an additional 30 percent, and the long program on Saturday night made up the remaining half. Sasha's *Swan Lake* routine was flawless. She placed first in her qualifying group even though she had left out a triple loop. (She had struggled with the jump and felt as if she had "lost" it just days before. Sasha was nervous to try the jump in competition, so Robin advised her to leave it out and just do a spiral instead.)

Next up was the short program. Again Sasha didn't crack under pressure. She hit all of her elements. Even though she didn't have a tricky triple-triple jump combination like some of the other skaters, she was first after the short. She even got four 6.0s from the judges for presentation. Sasha felt ready for her long, especially after watching videos of herself doing the triple loop. She got the jump back just in time for her long program.

Despite having skated so well and pacing herself, Sasha was nervous before her long program. All was going well until her takeoff for her triple salchow. She did a double instead. The mistake cost her. Sasha ended up taking home the silver. Japan's Shizuka Arakawa won the gold and Michelle Kwan the bronze.

---

66 *I've always looked up to [Michelle]. To be able to hold it together and skate a good program and beat Michelle was a big step.* 99

—SASHA ON BEATING MICHELLE KWAN

Sasha was sad not to have won. But at the same time, she was thrilled to win the silver—her first medal at Worlds. "It was really nice to stand up on the podium and see the U.S. flags up there and just be a part of the competition," Sasha wrote in her journal on her website. "There were so many strong performances in all the events. It was an amazing World Championships to be a part of."

The last event of the season was the Marshalls Challenge. Sasha wanted to end the season on a high note, but she was starting to feel run-down. Plus, she had started rehearsals for Champions on Ice. Still, Sasha performed better than she had all season, nailing seven triple jumps and taking home the gold. Best of all, Sasha received a standing ovation. The competition was the perfect end to a successful season.

Chapter | Eight

A Silver Finish

After touring with Champions on Ice and enjoying a few weeks of vacation in Italy with her family, Sasha needed to get back to training for the upcoming season. The USFSA had a few new rules. Women could wear pants when they skated and their short routines could be ten seconds longer than before. But more important, a new ISU scoring system, the Code of Points, was being phased in. It was set to be in place permanently by the 2005 World Championships. The new system was meant to be more exact and fair. Skaters would get points in the hundreds based on the difficulty and execution of each element they performed. Sasha and Robin studied the new rules to make sure they could make the most of the scoring system.

Sasha's new long program was set to a beautiful piece from *The Nutcracker,* a ballet with music by Pyotr Ilich Tchaikovsky. In her program, Sasha played young Clara on

Christmas Eve. Sasha was working on designs for her costume—she and Robin both loved fashion. Sasha's short program was set to "Dark Eyes," a familiar piece. Sasha had briefly used it for her short in the 2000–2001 season, before her back injury. She had always loved the music and was happy to use it again.

Despite all of her preparation, Sasha didn't feel that her skating was where it should be. One week before her first Grand Prix, Skate America, Sasha's back started hurting again. She immediately went to her doctor. After sitting out several competitions in October and November and undergoing intensive physical therapy for a few weeks, Sasha felt better.

Her season, however, did not improve. In early December, the airline lost her luggage before the Marshalls Pro Am. Sasha's skates were in her checked bag. She missed an entire day of practice before her luggage arrived. In the actual competition, Sasha's timing was off, and she fell three times.

On top of her skating difficulties, Sasha and the rest of the Cohens were homesick for California. They had finally settled into their new apartment that fall. But just before Christmas, the family decided to move back to the West Coast. Robin was very understanding. "[Robin] is a great coach and friend," Sasha wrote in her website journal. "Robin is supportive of my decision to move home to California to be back with my friends and family. I wish her nothing but the best in the future."

In early 2005, Sasha finished her autobiography, *Fire on Ice,* which she wrote with Amanda Maciel.

The next few weeks were a blur for Sasha. The Cohens stayed with friends for one week over the Christmas holiday. Then they moved to a rented apartment and once again began hunting for a house. The holiday season was busy enough, but Nationals were just weeks away. Sasha resumed training with John Nicks. The two fell into their old comfortable rhythm again. Sasha said it almost felt as if she had never left.

One thing that was different, however, was how much Sasha had learned from her other coaches. She had also learned about herself since leaving Nicks. Coming home seemed like the right decision for her. Her skating had improved, and performing in her new costumes put her in a great mood.

Despite the upheaval of the past month, Sasha felt ready for the 2005 Nationals, which were being held in Portland, Oregon. But shortly after checking into her hotel, Sasha learned some very sad news. Another skater, Angela Nikodinov, and her mother had been in a car accident. Angela was injured, and her mother had been killed. All the skaters were shocked. It was hard to feel that a skating event was important in comparison, but the competition began the next day. Sasha's short program went well, but she touched down on her triple lutz. She was determined that her long program be as clean as possible. In the end, she made two errors. She put her hand down on a triple loop and couldn't hang on after landing her lutz. But her performance was solid enough for a silver medal. She would be going to Worlds in Moscow, Russia.

Before Worlds, Sasha and Nicks kept busy training and adding elements to make her routines more competitive. Because of the new Code of Points system, Nicks and Sasha decided to rework some of the elements in her long program in order to squeeze in seven triple jumps. Sasha got on the plane to Russia determined to win the gold medal. It had been a difficult season, and she felt that she had a lot to prove to herself and her fans. But Sasha nearly lost her balance during her spiral sequence in the short program, and she had bobbles on several jumps in the long. In the end, she settled for second place, behind Irina Slutskaya. Although she was a little disappointed, it was hard to stay that way. Sasha was the only American on the medals podium, and she was proud of her performance.

The season was over, and it was time for Champions on Ice again. The other skaters on tour had become like a second family to Sasha. She enjoyed spending time skating, shopping, sightseeing, and going out to dinner with everyone. The tour was grueling, but it was also fun. Sasha especially liked performing her new routine to Barbra Streisand's "Don't Rain on My Parade." The upbeat music always made her smile, and she loved her beautiful turquoise costume.

In 2005 both Sasha and Nicks starred on separate reality television shows. Sasha appeared on *Project Runway*, where aspiring fashion designers created a skating costume for her. Nicks was a judge on the show *Skating with Celebrities*.

That summer, after returning home to California, Sasha bought a new town house with a view of the ocean, just a block and a half from the beach. Galina and Natasha, who had transferred back to a California high school, lived there with her as well. (Galina and Roger had separated in October 2004.) Sasha was proud to own her own house and had fun unpacking and decorating. After four homes in eighteen months, she hoped she could call it home for some time. She and her mom also took a cruise to Tahiti for some much needed rest and relaxation. Sasha knew the next season was going to require tremendous focus and energy. It was an Olympic year, and Sasha wanted a medal.

Sasha decided to continue training with Nicks, but first she made a trip to Connecticut. Although she enjoyed being back in California, ice time was harder to come by there. In Connecticut she spent a couple of months staying with a friend, pairs skater Garrett Lucash. She worked on her new long program with choreographer Nikolai Morozov. (Sasha had decided to keep "Dark Eyes" as her short program.)

The new long program was set to music from Franco Zeffirelli's 1968 film version of *Romeo and Juliet.* Sasha had used the music years earlier in an exhibition piece. She was excited to use it again in a different routine. "It's deep and emotional music, and I think it is perfect for me for the coming Olympic season," Sasha wrote in her journal. "Since the first time I heard *Romeo and Juliet,* I have always been in love with it. It's big, beautiful, and a very dramatic piece of music."

Sasha felt ready for the fall and the start of competition. Her costumes were being beaded, her routines were choreographed, and she felt fit and happy. She was so organized that she even had some free time on her hands. She decided to take some cooking classes at the nearby Laguna Culinary Arts school. Sasha learned how to cut and steam vegetables properly, trim meats, make sauces, and more. She enjoyed trying out what she learned in class at home in her own kitchen.

Sasha's first event of the 2005–2006 season was the Campbell's Classic. She was excited to try out her new program and get a better handle on the new scoring system, which she still didn't really understand. She landed seven triple jumps, but when her points showed up on the board, she had to ask Nicks if the numbers were good. Not only were they high, they were good enough for gold. "I've been nailing, like, 99 percent of what I do in practice. So that really gave me the confidence to do what I did," Sasha said.

❝I think [the new scoring system] is better for the reason that the skater and everyone else understands what's going on. There is a breakdown of what is rewarded and deducted for. It gives credit for all areas of skating and not just the jumps.❞

—SASHA ON THE NEW SCORING SYSTEM

Sasha returned home to rest and get ready for her next event—Skate America, which would take place in Atlantic City, New Jersey. But just a few days before the competition, Sasha tripped on the ice and fell. She landed on her hip and injured her groin muscles. She decided to withdraw from Skate America so she could heal and not jeopardize the second half of her season.

On top of her injury, Sasha got a cold that wouldn't go away. She was diagnosed with walking pneumonia (a lung infection) just days before her twenty-first birthday. Still, she had to celebrate such a big milestone. Galina threw Sasha a surprise party with fifty family members and friends. Galina made Sasha her favorite soufflé and brought a cake to the rink. Sasha also went out to dinner for sushi (one of her favorites).

Soon she was feeling well enough for her next event, the Trophée Eric Bompard, which was being held in Paris. Natasha accompanied Sasha. The sisters made it a point to try as many delicious Parisian desserts as possible. Sasha also managed to skate well, making just one mistake on a jump at the end of her long program. Next up was a fun twist on regular competition. In the Marshalls Challenge, the skaters performed two numbers and the audience—both in the crowd and at home—voted on a winner. Although Sasha came in second to Michelle Kwan, she had a fun time with the other skaters. It was a welcome break from the typical format of competitions.

As always, the holidays were busy for Sasha and her family. Sasha baked treats and hosted a big party at her house. She always had Nationals on her mind, which were in mid-January in St. Louis. After she returned from Nationals, she finally had a gold medal to go with all of her silvers. Sasha loved her gold and wanted more. "I'm looking for more than an Olympic medal," she said before the Games. "I want Olympic gold."

With her mind made up, Sasha had just a few weeks to get ready. This time, she was a favorite heading into the Olympics. The media was clamoring for her attention, but Sasha had decided not to give interviews until she arrived in Turin. She needed all of her focus to be on her training and tweaking her programs before the biggest competition of her life.

After arriving in Italy and making her way to the Olympic Village, Sasha met with reporters. The *Today Show*'s Katie Couric even took Sasha out for gelato (Italian ice cream). Most reporters were wondering if Sasha could finally deliver on the promise she had shown six years earlier when she was touted as Michelle Kwan's successor. "Everyone's career has a different trajectory. Everyone evolves in different ways. So far in my career I haven't been in the right place at the right time," Sasha said. "I've improved every year, but I just haven't put it all together yet. I plan on that this year."

To put her plan into action, Sasha knew she had to move out of the Olympic Village so she could stay focused. She decided to stay at a small hotel in Courmayeur, a village right on the France-Italy border. "I've matured and learned how to train," said Sasha. "I'm in control of my skating and I push myself. I know what I want and what I need to do to get it." She moved back into the Olympic Village just before the skating events began. She didn't march in the opening ceremonies or mingle much with the other athletes. Instead she decided to train, rest, and read.

When the day of her short program arrived, Sasha had twenty friends and family members in the stands to cheer her on. They had quite a wait, though. Sasha was the very last skater that evening. Sasha avoided watching the other skaters perform and focused on what she needed to do—skate a clean short program. She skated out on the ice in her turquoise costume with its flowery skirt and struck her opening pose to "Dark Eyes." Her first combination was a triple lutz–double toe loop. Sasha nailed it. With the confidence of a tricky jump combination completed, Sasha relaxed and got into the number, playing off the energy of the crowd. Her remaining jumps were all nearly perfect and her spins, footwork, and transitions were breathtaking. As the final note of music ended, the crowd roared its approval and was on its feet for a standing ovation.

Sasha stayed still, taking in the feeling of skating a great routine at the Olympics. Then she pumped her fist in celebration and skated around the rink. She smiled, blew kisses, and waved at fans before skating off to await her scores. "I really wanted to soak it in," she said. "Everyone is so quick to get off [the ice]. But we work so hard for this. It's nice to take two minutes to enjoy your accomplishments." Sasha had more reason to celebrate after she saw her scores. She was in first place. She led second-place Irina Slutskaya by three-hundredths of a point. That evening, Sasha celebrated until 3 A.M. with her family and friends.

The next day, she decided to rest, ice her aching muscles, and skip the practice sessions. The media immediately began speculating about Sasha's whereabouts. But she had learned not to care too much about what people were saying. She was on the ice Thursday morning, the day of her free skate. At the warm-up that evening, she felt ready for her *Romeo and Juliet* routine.

Sasha *was* ready—that is, until she started falling on the last few jumps of her warm-up. She was rattled, and her confidence started to crumble. Sasha did her best to compose herself before her program, and she felt better by the time she stood in the center of the ice minutes later. However, she fell on her first jump and touched down on the second. After just thirty seconds of skating, she felt her lead slip away. Yet somehow Sasha pulled herself together and skated an inspired remainder of the routine. She kept thinking positively, believing that she could finish the program without any more mistakes. "I knew I might have blown my chance for a medal, but I was incredibly proud of myself for finishing my program with grace and strength," Sasha later wrote in her autobiography.

When she left the ice, Sasha was stunned. So was the crowd. Sasha was in first place! All of the highest-ranked skaters were still left to perform, however, so Sasha was sure she wouldn't medal. Backstage, she took off her embroidered gold-and-burgundy skating dress and figured out what she was going to say to the media. Sasha was definitely disappointed, but she had no regrets.

After Irina Slutskaya, the last skater, finished her routine, Sasha was surprised to learn that she was in second place. None of the skaters had been perfect. Slutskaya had fallen as well. Sasha had won the silver medal! Sasha quickly pulled her dress back on. She headed for the podium to see the U.S. flag raised alongside the Japanese flag (honoring gold medalist Shizuka Arakawa) and the Russian flag (for bronze medalist Slutskaya). Her medal may not have been the color she had hoped for and dreamed of, but Sasha was an Olympic medalist!

Chapter | Nine

In the Spotlight

After winning the silver medal, Sasha was overwhelmed with media requests. She tried not to read all of the magazine and newspaper articles about herself. She didn't want to be influenced by what other people said, and some of the stories weren't very flattering. One reporter from the *Houston Chronicle* even called her "America's poster child for breathtaking talent and unfulfilled potential."

Although she avoided reading the papers, Sasha made it a point to watch all of her television interviews. She had fun seeing herself interviewed on shows, including *The Tonight Show with Jay Leno, The Ellen DeGeneres Show, Live with Regis and Kelly,* and *Jimmy Kimmel Live.* Sasha also got to attend some celebrity-filled parties, including two events leading up to the Academy Awards. Sasha met the stars and discussed her acting aspirations with them.

But before she could take any acting jobs, Sasha had to think about the World Championships, which were being held in Calgary, Canada. Although Sasha was the only Olympic medalist appearing at the event, she knew that the other skaters were talented. They were also mostly younger than Sasha, who at twenty-one was four and five years older than many of the teens competing.

❝You feel it when you're a little off in the air, and it's like: Uh-oh. When you fall you hear that 'ohhhhh' from the crowd, then a big hush. Which is how you feel inside, times a thousand. When you get up, you've lost a couple of seconds. The programs are jam-packed: You have to hold the spins for a certain amount of revolutions, hold your position on the spirals. There's nowhere to make up the time. The toll is more than falling on the jump. You'll lose points somewhere else too: You're going to be late for something—you choose what.❞

—SASHA ON FALLING

Sasha was in the lead after the short program, ahead of Japan's Fumie Suguri and U.S. teammate Kimmie Meissner. But once again, the long program plagued her. Sasha fell and tumbled to third place. She had to content herself with a bronze medal. To everyone's surprise, Meissner won the event after landing seven triples, including two triple-triple combinations. "I used to cry [when I didn't win gold]," Sasha told reporters after Worlds. "But I used up all my tears." It wasn't the way Sasha wanted to end her season, but she was ready to move on.

After a few much needed days off in Cozumel, Mexico, with her mother and Natasha, Sasha headed to Fort Meyers, Florida. She was starting rehearsals for her seventh-straight year with Champions on Ice. Sasha had a new exhibition program to the song "God Bless America," performed by Celine Dion. Her costume was a sparkly, beaded red-and-white halter dress.

The fan support on tour was especially important to Sasha after her year of ups and downs. On her website, she told her fans how much she valued their support. She also announced that she planned to keep skating and stay eligible for the 2010 Olympics. Many reporters had speculated that Sasha might retire after she hinted of her plans to begin acting.

Sasha was thrilled to get the chance to play herself on an episode of the television series *Las Vegas*. She was a big fan of actor Josh Duhamel. She even got to flirt with him as part of her role in the show. It turned out that Duhamel was a fan of Sasha's as well. "She's a natural," he said. "She didn't appear too nervous, but I guess this is nothing compared to the Olympics." The episode was filmed in April 2006. It aired in May. Sasha almost missed seeing the show because she was on tour. She stepped off the ice just seconds before she appeared on-screen.

Just weeks after her appearance on *Las Vegas,* Sasha got a part in the independent film (a movie not backed by a major motion picture studio) titled *Moondance Alexander.* It stars Don Johnson and Lori Loughlin. She learned how to ride a horse for her role as a snobby high school girl. Sasha also started taking acting lessons before she traveled to Calgary for filming. Sasha learned she loved acting almost as much as skating. In her online journal, Sasha wrote: "I can't begin to describe what it was like to learn lines, perform a role of another person, and be around such a creative cast. . . . The entire experience was awesome. One of the best things was being able to work with the other people in the cast." *Moondance Alexander* was set for a spring 2007 release.

Sasha has said her ideal partner if she was on *Skating with Celebrities* would be actor Josh Hartnett.

More acting roles soon came Sasha's way. She agreed to a guest appearance on the television show *CSI: NY* as well as to a role in the Will Ferrell figure-skating comedy *Blades of Glory,* which was being produced by Ben Stiller. She also had the role of the head cheerleader in *Bratz: The Movie,* which will be released in summer 2007.

In addition to acting, Sasha's other post-Olympic ambition was to travel as much as possible. Champions on Ice wrapped in August, and although she traveled nonstop with the tour, Sasha planned several relaxing vacations during her time off. She managed a week in Bora Bora in June and a week in Sun Valley, Idaho, in August.

The 2006–2007 skating season was fast approaching. Sasha was ready for another year. She skated at Campbell's Cup, a team event in Cincinnati, Ohio, in October. The crowd cheered her through her "Dark Eyes" routine, and she skated a great program.

In late 2006, Sasha made a surprise announcement. She was taking a year off from skating. Instead of defending her U.S. title, she wanted some time away from the intense demands of competition. She made it clear that she wasn't retiring but instead focusing on the 2009 Worlds in Los Angeles and the 2010 Olympics in Vancouver, Canada. "I love the thrill compe-tition brings and I'm not ready to give that up," said Sasha. "But I'm the type of person who is all or nothing. When I train and compete, it's my life. I can't be there just to be there."

Sasha continued to take acting lessons. She also appeared in a print ad for the American Milk Producers' Body by Milk campaign. Sasha had always wanted to be in a Got Milk? ad. She was even more excited when she arrived at the shoot and learned that the mustache was made with a mixture of milk and vanilla ice cream. Getting the right mustache meant lots of sips of a delicious milk shake! The end result was an advertisement Sasha was proud of. "I am very pleased to be part of a new promotion that encourages good nutrition and fitness," Sasha said. "I have always promoted good eating habits and exercise and want to be a role model for good health."

In 2006 Sasha auctioned off some of her skating memorabilia on eBay to raise money for charity.

Sasha also wants to be a role model for giving to others. She donates her time and money to various charities, including the Women's Sports Foundation, Girls Inc., Connecticut Children's Medical Center, and Soldiers' Angels. She has links to each of the organizations on her website and encourages her fans to get involved in these or other charities.

Despite the media claims that Sasha hasn't lived up to her potential, Sasha is one of the most winning skaters currently competing. Since 2003, she has finished in the top three in twenty consecutive competitions. She has a U.S. gold medal and two silvers, three World medals, and an Olympic silver. But her story isn't finished. The best of Sasha could be yet to come.

Enjoying the Journey

Atypical senior figure skater's career lasts six or seven years. At twenty-two, Sasha is older than most of her competitors, but she shows no signs of slowing down. She even plans on skating at the 2010 Olympic Games. "[Shizuka] Arakawa is proof that perseverance does pay off," Sasha said of the twenty-four-year-old Olympic gold medalist. "Maybe I'm a slow learner, but I'm still learning. And I find if I'm not skating, training, and competing, I don't have the same sense of accomplishment in my life. I don't feel like ending my career."

But skating is only one of the several careers Sasha could have. She has proven that she has acting talent, and she would like to pursue television and movie opportunities. She has modeled and enjoys designing costumes and clothing. Her book has also been revised and reprinted, and it keeps selling. While she would enjoy seeing where each of these interests could lead,

Sasha has said that her first love will always be figure skating.

Even if Sasha never wins a gold medal at Worlds or the Olympics, she has touched the sport with her strength, grace, and exquisite artistry. "I've had such an incredible journey in this process," Sasha said after the 2006 Olympics. "I've grown so much as a person and as an athlete. I've become stronger, tougher than I think I am, and I have to be proud of all those things and take them with me to whatever I choose to do."

PERSONAL STATISTICS

Name:

Alexandra Pauline Cohen

Nicknames:

Sasha

Born:

October 26, 1984

Birthplace:

Los Angeles, California

Height:

5' 2"

Weight:

95 lbs.

CAREER STATISTICS

Year	Competition	Finish
1998	U.S. National Championships, Novice	2nd
1999	U.S. National Championships, Junior	2nd
2000	U.S. National Championships	2nd
2000	World Junior Championships	6th
2002	U.S. National Championships	2nd
2002	Olympic Games	4th
2002	World Championships	4th
2003	U.S. National Championships	3rd
2003	World Championships	4th
2004	U.S. National Championships	2nd
2004	World Championships	2nd
2005	U.S. National Championships	2nd
2005	World Championships	2nd
2006	U.S. National Championships	1st
2006	Olympic Games	2nd
2006	World Championships	3rd

GLOSSARY

axel jump: a jump in which the skater takes off forward from one foot and spins in the air to land on the other foot going backward. Most female skaters do a double axel (which is actually two and a half revolutions), while male skaters often do triples.

combination: two or more jumps in a row. As soon as the first jump is landed, a skater starts performing the second.

edge: the outside or inside of a skating blade

flip jump: a jump in which a skater pushes off the back inside edge of the skate while digging the toe pick of the opposite foot into the ice and lands on the picking foot

footwork: a required element that involves fast, connected steps across the surface of the ice. Points are deducted if a skater's footwork is sloppy or does not cover the ice.

long program: also called the free skate. It features a skater's artistic or creative moves, and there are no required elements. For women, the long program is four minutes long and for men, four and a half minutes.

loop jump: a jump that begins on the back outside edge of a skater's blade and ends with a landing on the same back outside edge. If the skater uses a toe pick to get started in the revolutions, the jump is called a toe loop.

lutz jump: a jump in which a skater takes off from the back outside edge, using the toe pick of the opposite foot to launch into the air, and lands on the back outside edge of the picking foot

salchow jump: a jump that starts off on the back inside edge and ends on the back outside edge of the other foot

short program: this two-and-a-half-minute routine calls on the skater to perform eight required elements in any order the skater chooses

spiral: a move that shows off control, speed, and flexibility. A skater extends one leg behind as high as it can go and glides across the ice with all of the weight on the inside or outside edge of the other skate.

toe pick: the small, jagged teeth on the front of the figure skating blade

SOURCES

2 Scott M. Reid, "Cohen Battles Through Flu to Challenge for Olympic Berth," *Orange County Register*, January 13, 2006.

3 John Crumpacker, "Figure Skating: Cohen's Short Program All But Ices Olympic Spot," *San Francisco Chronicle*, January 13, 2006.

4 Mark Starr, "It's Sasha's Turn," *Newsweek*, January 23, 2006, 50.

4–5 Crumpacker, "Figure Skating: Cohen's Short Program All But Ices Olympic Spot."

7 Sasha Cohen with Amanda Maciel, *Fire on Ice: Autobiograhy of a Champion Figure Skater*, (New York: Harper Collins, 2005), 8.

9 Ibid., 13–14.

10–11 Ibid., 16.

12 Ibid., 19.

16 Ibid., 24.

18 Ibid., 25–26.

20 Mark Emmons, "Sasha Cohen, 15, Takes Center Stage," *Orange County Register*, February 12, 2000.

23 Cohen, *Fire on Ice*, 35.

27 Scott M. Reid, "Sasha Cohen: Rebel With a Cause," *Orange County Register*, January 7, 2002.

27–28 Emmons, "Sasha Cohen, 15, Takes Center Stage."

29 E.M. Swift, "No. 2 With a Bullet," *Sports Illustrated*, February 21, 2000, 66.

32 Cohen, *Fire on Ice*, 58.

32 Philip Hersh, "Not Bashful About Getting Her Way: Sasha Cohen, 17, has skill and confidence to challenge Kwan," *Chicago Tribune*, January 11, 2002.

36–37 Ibid.

37 Reid, "Sasha Cohen: Rebel With a Cause."

38 Ibid.

39 Hersh, "Not Bashful About Getting Her Way."

40 Linda Robertson, "Michelle Kwan is in First, but Cohen Steals the Show," *The Miami Herald*, January 11, 2002.

40 Philip Hersh, "Cut Sasha Cohen a Little Bit of Slack," *Chicago Tribune*, January 29, 2002.

41 Cohen, *Fire on Ice*, 77.

44 Ibid., 85.

44 Mark Emmons, "Fiery Cohen Could Crash Figure Skating Podium Party," *Toronto Star*, February 18, 2002.

45 Reid, "Rebel With a Cause."

45 Jeff Zilgitt, "Sasha and Sarah Show Their Youth is a Force to Reckon With," *USA Today*, February 20, 2002.

46 Reid, "Rebel With a Cause."

46 Zilgitt, "Sasha and Sarah Show Their Youth is a Force to Reckon With."

47 Reid, "Rebel With a Cause."

48 Scott M. Reid, "Cohen's Moment Arrives," *Orange County Register*, February 21, 2002.

48 Ibid.

49 Emmons, "Fiery Cohen Could Crash Figure Skating Podium Party."

51 Cohen, *Fire on Ice*, 106.

54 Philip Hersh, "Sasha Cohen's Coach-Switching Move is Baffling," *Chicago Tribune*, August 22, 2002.

55 Christine Brennan, "Cohen Can Still Fulfill Skating Promise," *USA Today*, November 1, 2002.

55 Ibid.

57 Cathy Harasta, "Cohen Sees This a 'Year of Opportunity,'" *Dallas Morning News*, January 14, 2003.

57 Vicki Micahaelis, "Cohen, Weiss Stand Out as Favorites," *USA Today*, January 16, 2003.

58 Ibid.

58 Cohen, *Fire on Ice*, 119.

60 Jo-Ann Barnas, "Cohen Better Handling Ice Pressure," *Detroit Free Press*, March 27, 2003.

62 Harasta, "Cohen Sees This a 'Year of Opportunity.'"

64 Cohen, *Fire on Ice*, 131.

67 Philip Hersh, "Cohen Hires New Coach," *Chicago Tribune*, December 24, 2003.

68   Ibid.
68   F. Fitzpatrick, "Cohen's Connection with Her Coach Took Her to New Heights," *Philadelphia Inquirer*, March 30, 2004.
69   Ibid.
69   Hersh, "Cohen Hires New Coach."
70   Linda Robertson, "Cohen Takes Aim on Next Level," *Miami Herald*, January 3, 2004.
73   Christine Brennan, "Cohen Must Put Her Mind at Ease," *USA Today*, January 9, 2004.
74   Shawn Nicholls, "Sasha Cohen: Look Out, World," *Sports Illustrated for Kids*, January 1, 2004, 46.
74–75 Sasha Cohen, "Thanks for All Your Support, Especially the E-mails," *SashaCohen.com*, April 1, 2004, http://www.sashacohen.com/journal.shtml (February 19, 2007).
77   Sasha Cohen, "I'm Returning Home and Will Train with Mr. Nicks," *SashaCohen.com*, December 22, 2004, http://www.sashacohen.com/journal.shtml (February 19, 2007).
81   Sasha Cohen, "I Have Always Loved *Romeo and Juliet*," *SashaCohen.com*, August 25, 2005, http://www.sashacohen.com/journal.shtml (February 19, 2007).
82   Gary Mihcoes, "Cohen Separates Herself from the Field," *USA Today*, October 10, 2005.
82   Alice Park, "10 Questions for Sasha Cohen," *Time*, January 9, 2006, 6.
83–84 Alice Park, "The Ice Storm," *Time*, February 6, 2006, 48.
84   E. M. Swift, "Her Time Has Come," *Sports Illustrated*, February 6, 2006, 74.
84   Sasha Cohen, "Mr. Nicks is a Calming Influence, Today's a Good Start," *SashaCohen.com*, March 16, 2005, http://www.sashacohen.com/journal.sthml (April 11, 2007).
85   Amy Shipley, "Cohen Is Out Late, Up Early," *The Washington Post*, February 22, 2006.
86   Cohen, *Fire on Ice*, 205.

88   David Barron, "Two Early Slip-Ups Put Cohen's Dream of a Gold Medal on Ice," *Houston Chronicle*, February 24, 2006.
89   "Falling on Your Butt," *Sports Illustrated*, February 27, 2006, 38.
90   "For the Record," *Sports Illustrated*, April 3, 2006, 22.
90–91 Olivia Abel, et al. "Las Vegas on Ice," *People*, May 1, 2006, 28.
91   Sasha Cohen, "It Was Fun Playing a Mean Girl in *Moondance Alexander*," *SashaCohen.com*, August 5, 2006, http://www.sashacohen.com/journal.sthml (February 19, 2007).
92   "Sasha Cohen Withdraws from 2007 State Farm U.S. Figure Skating Championships," *USFigureSkating.org*, December 22, 2006, http://www.usfigureskating.org/event_story.asp?id=37059 (February 19, 2007).
93   Sasha Cohen, "Got Milk? Photo Shoot Was Way Too Cool!" *SashaCohen.com*, September 3, 2006, http://www.sashacohen.com/journal.sthml (February 19, 2007).
95   E.M. Swift, "Silver Lining," *Sports Illustrated*, March 6, 2006, 42.
96   Barron, "Two Early Slip-Ups Put Cohen's Dream of a Gold Medal on Ice."

BIBLIOGRAPHY

Books

Cohen, Sasha, with Amanda Maciel. *Fire on Ice: Autobiography of a Champion Figure Skater.* New York: HarperCollins, 2005.

Freese, Joan. *Play-by-Play Figure Skating.* Minneapolis: Lerner Publications Company, 2004.

Selected Articles

Emmons, Mark. "Sasha Cohen, 15, Takes Center Stage," *Orange County Register,* February 12, 2000.

Reid, Scott M. "Sasha Cohen: Rebel with a Cause." *Orange County Register,* January 7, 2002.

Swift, E. M. "Her Time Has Come." *Sports Illustrated,* February 6, 2006, 74–77.

Swift, E. M. "Silver Lining." *Sports Illustrated,* March 6, 2006, 42–44.

WEBSITES

International Skating Union

http://www.isu.org

The International Skating Union oversees many skating competitions—including figure skating and speed skating. It runs the Grand Prix series and the World Championships. Its site offers results of recent competitions, information about rules, and a photo gallery.

SashaCohen.com

http://www.sashacohen.com

Sasha's official website features her profile, competitive highlights, journal, and other things related to Sasha.

U.S. Figure Skating Online

http://www.usfsa.org

The official website of the United States Figure Skating Association features skaters' biographies, career statistics, and season highlights.

INDEX

MONTVILLE TWP. PUBLIC LIBRARY
90 HORSENECK ROAD
MONTVILLE, NJ 07045